Open Learning Guide 2

How to Help Learners Assess Their Progress: writing objectives, self-assessment questions and activities

Roger Lewis

CET Council for Educational Technology

Published and distributed by the Council for Educational Technology, 3 Devonshire Street, London W1N 2BA

First published 1984
ISBN 0 86184–124–7

British Library Cataloguing in Publication Data

Lewis, Roger *1944–*
    How to help learners assess their progress.
    — (Open learning guide; 2)
    1. Text books–Authorship   2. Distance education   3. Students, Self-rating of
    I. Title   II. Series
    371.3′2   LB3045.5

ISBN 0 86184–124–7

Printed in Great Britain by H Charlesworth & Co Ltd
254 Deighton Road
Huddersfield HD2 1JJ

Contents

Preface   vii

Introduction   1
Open-Learning Guides   1
What this book covers   2
Acknowledgements   3

SECTION ONE. HOW TO WRITE OBJECTIVES   5
How to write objectives   7
Contents   7
Introduction   7
Getting to the objectives   9
Writing objectives   11
Wording objectives for the learner   14
Ensuring a range and variety of objectives   19

SECTION TWO. HOW TO WRITE SELF-ASSESSMENT
QUESTIONS AND ACTIVITIES   27
How to write self-assessment questions and activities   29
Contents   29
Introduction   29
The importance of self-assessment questions and activities   30
Writing self-assessment questions   35
Different types of SAQ   43
Writing the activities   58

SECTION THREE. OTHER MEANS OF HELPING LEARNERS
TO ASSESS THEIR PROGRESS   63
Other means of helping learners to assess their progress   65
Contents   65
Self-help groups   65
A tutor   66
Face-to-face sessions   74
New technology   77

SECTION FOUR. CHECKLISTS, BOOKLIST AND
GLOSSARY   83

Checklists   85
Introduction   85
Checklists   85
Booklist   90
Objectives   90
Assessment   90

Glossary   92

APPENDICES   95

Appendix 1. Summary: good and bad objectives   97
Appendix 2. Writing tutor-assessed questions   99
Appendix 3. Writing multiple-choice questions   102

Preface

Since 1975 the Council for Educational Technology has been continuously involved in the development of open-learning systems. The first stages of this work concentrated on 'non-advanced further education' and enabled the Council to make a major contribution to the National Extension College's 'FlexiStudy' system and other early developments, and incidentally to provide much advice and practical help in the form of publications and training workshops to lecturers who were finding their way into the new field of open learning. This experience ·allied to that of the Open University– helped to provide the foundation upon which the 'Open Tech' programme ·Manpower Services Commission– and PICKUP initiative ·Department of Education and Science– are built, has led to the much more flexible approach now being taken by the Business and Technician Education Councils and other validating bodies, and is recognized by the contract given to the Council by MSC to provide a training and support unit for Open Tech projects.

Maintaining the momentum of its work in open learning, the Council has moved into the fields of supported self-study in secondary schools and informal adult learning. In all this work over the past nine years, the Council has benefited from the cooperation and personal experience of an increasingly large group of experienced specialists in open learning and has, through its publications, attempted to make this experience available to lecturers, trainers and teachers who found themselves confronted with the need to get involved in open-learning methods.

This new series of Open Learning Guides is a further move in making the accumulated experience of those who have developed open-learning methods in the United Kingdom available to newcomers to the field. The series editor, Roger Lewis, has taken a lead in developments both through his work for the National Extension College and through his involvement from the beginning with the Council's own work. The drafts of the Guides have been commented on and improved by a process of consultation with several experts in the open-learning network, with the intention that the result will be a series of books which are directly helpful to those in industry, the professions, and adult, further and higher education who are called upon to develop and run open-learning schemes.

Norman Willis
Assistant Director
Council for Educational Technology
April 1984

Introduction

OPEN–LEARNING GUIDES
This series of books is intended as a practical help to people setting up open-learning schemes whether in education or training. The advice is deliberately aimed across the whole range of schemes and levels. The structure of the series is as follows.

WHAT IS OPEN LEARNING?

OPEN LEARNING IN ACTION

HOW TO DEVELOP AND MANAGE AN OPEN-LEARNING SCHEME	HOW TO TUTOR AND SUPPORT LEARNERS	HOW TO FIND AND ADAPT MATERIALS AND CHOOSE MEDIA

HOW TO HELP LEARNERS ASSESS THEIR PROGRESS: HOW TO WRITE OBJECTIVES, SELF-ASSESSMENT QUESTIONS AND ACTIVITIES

HOW TO COMMUNICATE WITH THE LEARNER

HOW TO MANAGE THE PRODUCTION PROCESS

The Guides thus cover the three main parts of most schemes: a management system, a tutorial support system and learning materials. Each book stands on its own but there are many areas of overlap and reference is made to other volumes in the series. In particular you are recommended to consult Volume 1, *Open Learning in Action* as you use this text.

All the volumes except *Open Learning in Action* contain open-learning features. These include:

— objectives
— quiz sections which act as summaries
— activities to enable you to apply your learning to your work
— checklists to guide you whilst working through the activities
— the provision of frequent examples to show how the ideas have been applied in particular cases.

These features are indicated in the text by introductory symbols to make them easily recognizable. *Key words for this volume are defined in the Glossary in Section 4.*

WHAT THIS BOOK COVERS

This book deals with the early part of one suggested sequence for preparing a learning package. This sequence is outlined in Volume 5, *How to Develop and Manage an Open-Learning Scheme*, and discussed more fully in Volume 6, *How to Communicate With the Learner*. It consists of the following stages: firstly, write objectives; secondly, prepare assessment questions and activities, together with discussion or responses; thirdly, write the linking text (or its equivalent in another medium).

The first two stages provide a clear structure for the third and make relevant and disciplined text more likely. This book deals with the first two stages — writing objectives and setting assessment questions and activities. Writing the text is covered in Volume 6.

This is only *one* sequence. It is possible to set about the task in a range of other ways. We now know better than to insist on one sequence as the correct one. In particular, some planners and writers prefer to work their way round to setting objectives only after some drafting of text has actively been carried out. Others again prefer to experiment with assessment questions and then to work back to writing the objectives.

This book is organized in the following way.

Section 1: how to write objectives

Section 2: how to write self-assessment questions and activities

Section 3: other means of helping learners to assess their progress (such as self-help groups, a tutor, face-to-face sessions, and new technologies)

Section 4: checklists, booklists and glossary

The second part of the book is the largest. Several very sound sources already exist on how to write objectives. You are referred to these at appropriate points. But assessment in open learning, and particularly self-assessment and activities, are not nearly so well covered elsewhere and writers of self-instructional materials often find it difficult to think up interesting, challenging and relevant questions. Hence the greater length of Section 2.

I cover assessment issues only so far as they relate to open learning. This is not a treatment of assessment more generally, so there is no discussion of formal assessment (eg, merits of continuous versus summative assessment, how to set formal examinations). Help with these matters can be found elsewhere (see the Booklist). My concern is with the informal feedback on performance that the open learner needs in order to make progress and in particular with the process by which he may be helped to become his own assessor.

Objectives

As a result of this book you should be able to build into your package features that help your target learners to assess their progress, ie:

— appropriate objectives
— effective self-assessment questions and activities
— suitable responses to the questions and activities
— (if appropriate) tutor-marked questions and ancillary notes for tutors
— (if appropriate) materials to help structure any face-to-face sessions.

In addition you should be alert to the possibilities of using new technologies such as computers to help your learners to assess their progress. You will also have practised the first two steps of writing learning materials, ie:

— writing objectives
— writing self-assessment questions, activities and responses.

More detailed contents of each section and related objectives appear in the introductions to each of the three sections.

ACKNOWLEDGEMENTS
As with other volumes in this series, the manuscript of this book was submitted to a team of readers who made many helpful comments for which I am grateful. The readers were

John Coffey
Rob Littlejohn
Gaye Manwaring
Nigel Paine

Phil Race
Frances Robertson
Doug Spencer
Philip Waterhouse
Bob Windsor

Bob Windsor, Clive Neville and Lesley MacDonald managed the project for the Council for Educational Technology and Muriel Pashley edited this and the other volumes in the series. I should like to thank them for their ready cooperation at all times.

I am grateful to Richard Freeman of the National Extension College and Bob Windsor of CET for advice on the section dealing with new technology, and to Janet Bollen of NEC putting the typescript into its final form.

Roger Lewis
April 1984

Section One. How to Write Objectives

How to write objectives

CONTENTS
Introduction
Getting to the objectives
Writing objectives
Wording objectives for the learner
Ensuring a range and variety of objectives

This section shows how you can get from general aims to more specific statements of what your learners will achieve; it gives hints on writing objectives and on phrasing them appropriately for your audience. It also suggests ways of ensuring range and variety in your objectives. Activities are provided to give you a chance to practise; checklists offer further guidance.

Objectives

By working through this section you should be able to:

— write objectives that help you to plan and write your package
— rephrase your objectives, if necessary, to communicate them to your learners
— locate and use sources of further help in writing objectives if you need them.

INTRODUCTION

Millions of words have been written about objectives. The topic generates not only words but also confusion and strong feeling. Fortunately this is not another text on the theory of objectives, on whether or not they are necessary, or on what they are. I assume that you are committed to using objectives, in one form or another, in your open-learning course. This is intended as a practical guide to help you to decide what sort of objectives you need and then how to write them.

If you are *not* convinced that objectives are necessary, or if you want to explore the territory in a more philosophical way, then I suggest that you read one of the sources recommended in the Booklist. You may also like to look at Volume 5 in this series of Guides which discusses the role of objectives in planning a course.

What is certain is that, rightly or wrongly, objectives are becoming more and more important, not only in training — which has always used them — but also in parts of the educational system that have, until now, been unaccustomed to their use, as the following extracts show.

paraphrase

'The schools can do their work better if they have
clear objectives about what should be learned and
these objectives are endorsed by all those whom they
serve... Clear and accepted descriptions of what
pupils should learn add meaning to the notion of
educational standards: before we try to raise
standards, we would do well to define them.
    I intend to work towards a published and broadly
agreed definition of the objectives of the main
subjects - what pupils should get out of the study
of each, and what level of attainment should be
expected at various stages and levels of ability,
over what range and in what depth...
    With the help of explicit objectives for the
main parts of the curriculum, it should be possible
to devise examination syllabuses and assessments
which give a reasonable assurance that a pupil awarded
a particular grade knows, understands and can do
certain things.'

Extract from a speech by Sir Keith Joseph quoted in 'The Times', 9 January 1983

In Scotland the 16 - 18 Action Plan involves
redesigning the curriculum into modules. Each
module centres on four or five learning outcomes.
These are linked to performance criteria which show
the level of competence required. The learning
outcomes direct

- content
- learning approach, and
- assessment.

Statement by Frances Robertson, Professional Tutor at Telford College of Further Education

In any interaction between tutor and learner, learner and learning material, there are outcomes. These vary considerably. Some are desirable, some undesirable; some are observable and some cannot easily be observed; some are important and some are trivial. And some are planned, some unplanned. An objective is a statement of an *intended* outcome; it is a description of what the learner should be able to do after following a particular course. It is thus planned. As we shall see, it should also be desirable, observable and important. Other outcomes will also occur and not all of them will be welcome. Learning remains a messy business. But thought given to objectives can make the process more manageable for the learner who then has some basis for measuring his progress.

GETTING TO THE OBJECTIVES

Volume 5 of the Open Learning Guides series shows how, during the process of course design, aims can be translated and refined into more specific statements of what it is hoped will be learned. This process can be expressed in the following way:

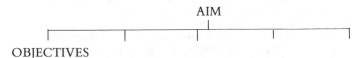

AIM

OBJECTIVES

This is the simplest way to work. Some designers use an interim level between aim and objective; others use different terms (eg, 'goal' instead of 'aim' and 'specific objective' instead of 'objective'). But the process of refinement is the same.

Sometimes, especially in training, it is possible to say that by achieving all the objectives the learner will realize exactly the aim of the course designer, as in the following example.

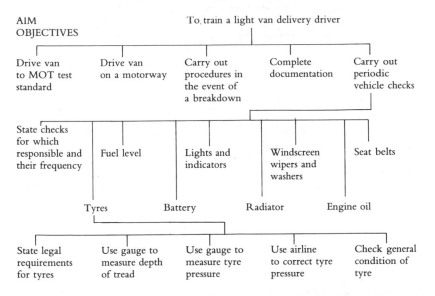

By mastering the sub-objectives (only samples have been given) the learner masters the objectives and thus should be able to handle most eventualities. If you are involved in training and need to explore this further then you should look at Dean and Whitlock's book (see Booklist on p 90).

But many readers will find this method over-formal and offputting. This will almost certainly be your reaction if, for example, you work in schools or in curricular areas where feelings and judgements play a big part; in teaching literature for example, or training health care professionals.

We were constrained also in the early days by trying to use behavioural objectives as the basis of our course planning. Hours were spent trying to persuade colleagues to use this approach which proved, in the end, unhelpful as a basis for writing. Much professional training, such as youth work, teaching and social work, is based on aims and procedures which are broad and value-laden. An example of an objective from our first module is: 'the student will be able to make and maintain professional interpersonal relationships and analyse relationships professionally encountered'. This objective does need to be further clarified, for example:

— the course team need to know the types of conditions under which such relationships may be made and maintained
— the course team and the examiners need to be clearly agreed on what is to count as 'professional' and 'analysis'.

However, tight analysis into sub-objectives is not possible because, for example:

— the range of conditions and personalities is too wide
— the boundaries of 'professional' are not clearly delimited
— rigorous assessment is not possible
— the values implicit in such an objective cannot be expressed purely in terms of objectives.

We spent a lot of time coming to terms with the difficulties and in working out how to use objectives for middle-range planning.

Extract from 'The YMCA Distance-Learning Scheme' in 'Open Learning in Action' (Volume 1 in this series)

If you are in this position then a different route may be more useful. This is to take your aim and then to write down some samples of the behaviour the learner would show that would, to you, prove that you were succeeding. Let's again take an example.

Aim
To help the social worker to realize that allocating resources involves making value judgements.
Sample objectives
The social worker will be able to:
— identify value issues present in particular case studies
— play various roles in a case conference, considering the relative claims of several clients
— analyse his own case-load and explain why resources have been allocated to particular clients.

This kind of objective is particularly appropriate when the course is teaching skills or capacities which in a sense are never totally and finally achieved, such as 'to think critically', 'to communicate effectively', 'to manage'. Hence, the objectives can only select outcomes which show an appropriate step towards such broader outcomes. You will, incidentally, then be particularly interested in activities as a means by which the learner can be helped to check his progress — see page 58.

```
(This is the first of two items on Observation: the second is
in Workpack 3.)
When you have finished this item you should be able to
recognize and accept that observation is an active process,
involving activities like selecting and classifying.
     You should be beginning to see the kinds of problems this
could cause in your professional observations - observing
people and behaviour is the main topic of the Workpack 3
item.
```

Extract from the YMCA Certificate in Youth and Community Work. Workpack 2. Induction Module WP2/2 p 1. Published by the YMCA National College

What matters is that you break the aim down into whatever objectives make most sense to you.

This, then, is the first suggested stage of writing a package: break learning down into objectives that are convenient for you to deal with.

A Activity

Look at your own course. Take your aims and turn them into objectives either by

— breaking each aim into objectives which together will add up exactly to achieve that aim, or by
— listing outcomes which will show the learner's progress towards your aim, or by other means of your own.

You should by now have some objectives to work on. The next section shows how to polish them.

WRITING OBJECTIVES

Objectives are, then, statements of what the learner will be able to do (outcomes) rather than of what the writer aims to do (intentions). This emphasis on what the learner will be able to *do* leads us to see that the most important part of an objective is the verb that begins it. It has to be specific enough to describe the behaviour that the successful learner will show.

Some verbs are vague and open to many interpretations. Where possible these should be avoided to make way for verbs that are more precise and which lead to observable behaviour.

✗	✓
to know	to list
to understand	to label
to appreciate	to distinguish between

Here are some examples, taken from a writers' workshop, that show an acceptable level of precision for the target audiences.

Target audience	*Examples of objectives*
Householders wishing to save energy and reduce fuel costs	You will be able to: — calculate the running costs of your electrical appliances — identify sources of heat loss in your home
Beginners to sailing	You will be able to: — explain the dangers of sailing a boat downwind — describe the procedure for righting a capsized boat
Cyclists aged 10–14	You will be able to: — carry out safety checks before riding your bike

C Checklist

Look back over your objectives. Are the verbs that begin them precise enough?

I have stressed the importance of the verb. If this is right then the outcome is usually defined clearly enough for most purposes. But if you are in training then you might want to go further and qualify the statement of what the learner will do. You may, for example, want to describe
— what the learner will be given to undertake a particular task (conditions)
— how well the learner will be expected to perform the task (standards).

Such objectives are particularly important when the desired outcome is for all learners to perform alike at a specified minimum level. Here are some examples of objectives which include all three elements, ie, behaviour, conditions and standards.

Behaviour	Conditions	Standards
The learner will solve correctly	given a calculator	eight out of ten of the problems.
The learner will derive	from a specified aim	a minimum of three clearly related objectives.
The learner will translate	given a 200-word passage from an O-level French text	with fewer than ten errors.

The rigid compartmentalizing of behaviour, conditions, and standards, is not always necessary. What is important is that the objective should state — in as precise terms as are appropriate — the performance required. Thus, to take the earlier example of the cycle, the objective may be: 'Carry out all the safety checks listed in "A Highway Code for Children"' (standard and reference added).

If you need to write objectives of this kind, or would like more practice in developing the verbs you use to describe learning outcomes, then there are several sources of simple and effective advice. Any one of the following will teach you quickly and painlessly.

Robert J Mager, *Preparing Instructional Objectives*, Fearon, 1962. Obtainable from bookshops.

Royal Air Force School of Education, *A Guide to the Writing of Objectives*, two volumes, one of which comprises a post-test and answers. (No date.) This would be very suitable for industrial trainers, but is not generally available.

T J Russell, *A Workshop on Writing Learning Objectives*, Coombe Lodge Further Education Staff College Working Paper 1331, January 1979. This is published in three versions for teachers/trainers in social work *or* business studies *or* technical subjects. Copies are obtainable from The Librarian, Coombe Lodge FE Staff College, Blagdon, Bristol BS18 6RG. The Coombe Lodge booklets would be particularly suitable for teachers in further education and higher education.

Activity

Consider whether it would help your learners to include reference in the objectives to conditions and/or standards of performance.

If so, add these.

If you need more practice then work through one of the sources suggested above. They are all themselves in open-learning format and you'll need to find only a couple of hours to benefit from them, together with practising on your own objectives.

Many of you will not need to go even so far as to add conditions or standards; the verb will be enough. But if you want to go further into the ramifications of objective formats then I suggest you read Chapter 3 of Briggs (see Booklist on p 90).

So it is possible to write objectives to a simple or to a much more complex format. The key is to make your objectives as specific as you need them to be in order to communicate to the desired audience, whether this is writers, planners, editors, potential learners or tutors (and, as we shall see, objectives may need to be spelled out in different ways for different users). There is no point in writing elaborate objectives that do not in fact succeed in communicating or which actually have the reverse effect and put people off. Decide on the format that is right for your scheme, explain it to your writers and train them to use it. Then make sure everyone keeps to the same format throughout.

Be prepared to spend time drafting and redrafting objectives. This will be time well spent as it will make the later stages of writing the text much easier. Writing workshops are a good way to generate objectives, to show them to colleagues for criticism and then to redraft. Failing that, use a colleague as a sounding board. It's also a good idea to try your objectives out on potential learners.

WORDING OBJECTIVES FOR THE LEARNER

Objectives serve the needs of a variety of people. They help *writers* to decide

— what content to include
— how to present the content
— what assessment questions to ask.

They help *counsellors* to advise intending learners on what skills a course will develop. They provide a basis for *tutors* to comment on learner assignments. They make it easier for all concerned to communicate: course planners with writers, writers with one another, planners with tutors.

But most of all they help *learners*. They help learners to see what skills a particular course intends to develop and whether or not these are relevant. They help the learner to plan his work and to take on responsibility for his own learning, and they help him to check progress towards achieving the aim of the course.

To do this the objectives need to be stated in a way that communicates with the learner. Sometimes objectives developed for writers and planners are too refined and sophisticated for the learner. At least two major current open-learning initiatives, the Pan Breakthrough series and the Irish Training Authority (AnCO) modules on marketing, ask their writers to produce objectives phrased in two different ways for the two audiences: editors and learners. The objectives have become softer and more welcoming by the time they reach the learner.

The specific objectives of the unit, *'A slice of the cake'* . . . *fractions*, are as follows.

After studying the unit, the reader should be able to:

(1) define the terms: numerator, denominator, fraction, proper fraction, improper fraction and mixed number

(2) add, subtract, multiply and divide proper fractions which have the same denominators and which have different denominators

(3) add, subtract, multiply and divide improper fractions which have the same denominators and which have different denominators

(4) change improper fractions into mixed numbers and vice versa

(5) simplify fractions by cancellation

(6) identify equivalent fractions

(7) calculate 'the whole' from a given fraction

(8) demonstrate by simple examples of your own why the rules for 2, 3, 4, and 5 work.

Objectives for planner/editor (in draft)

Some writers/editors decide not to include any separate and explicit mention of 'objectives' at all in the final text but use instead a variety of devices that carry out a similar function. These may be headed 'Introduction', 'Some questions to consider' or, as in the example on p 16, 'Preview'.

3 | A slice of the cake: fractions

Preview

Chapter 3 covers those fractions which you may meet in your home or working life. People tend to think that when they leave school or college they also leave fractions behind in the classroom. That isn't so.

You may work for an industrial company such as a car manufacturer; this company will buy steel and cut it into smaller lengths. Perhaps you are employed in the retailing field – many retail shops deal with wholesalers, whose job is to 'break bulk' by buying in large quantities and then dividing these large amounts into quantities which are a fraction of the size. People who work in a wages department or office often use fractions to work out overtime payments – 'time and a quarter', 'time and a half' are examples of the types of fractions used. Even farmers will use fractions, when they calculate what fraction of their land to use for different crops and animals.

These are only a few instances of where fractions are found. It's quite important, therefore, to be able to use them. They are not very popular with a lot of people, but they're not as difficult as some make them out to be.

Before studying this chapter, you should be able to add, subtract, multiply and divide whole numbers.

Once you have read through the chapter, and worked through the questions and activities, you should feel quite at ease using fractions. After explaining what a fraction is, the chapter will show how to add, subtract, multiply and divide them and how to deal with awkward fractions (such as 'improper' fractions, or fractions and whole numbers mixed). The chapter will show the basic rules for dealing with fractions in a range of different problems.

Extract from 'Making Numbers Work' by D Floyd (Pan Breakthrough Series), pp 58, 59, 1982. In the final version the objectives are deliberately softened for motivational purposes

Block 3, Unit 1   **THE GP AND THE SHOP ASSISTANT**

In this unit we look at the work of the doctor and the shop assistant, two very different occupations, differently rewarded. Our discussion leads us to consider the concepts of 'class' and 'status'. You read some more of your set book with the purpose of answering specific questions and you practise again the skill of 'brainstorming'.

'Check your learning' can be found on page 63.

Extract from 'Preparing for Social Science' by L Maynard and R Lewis, p 57, National Extension College, 1981

Unit 2   **Introducing Coordinates**

Introduces rectangular x- and y-coordinates, including plotting points on coordinate grids.

TEC Maths Bank objectives BB2.

You will need squared paper for this Unit.

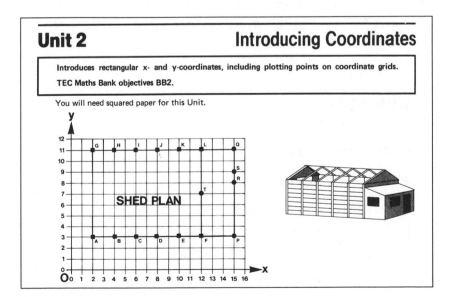

Extract from 'FLEXIMATHS' by J Gillespie, Volume 1, p 18, National Extension College, 1982

WORDPOWER UNIT 2

THE INTERVIEW

Introduction

This unit is intended to help you plan for an interview — thinking about what you will say, what you want to find out, what it feels like to be both interviewer and interviewed.

Contents

Your previous interviews   12

Organising yourself for an interview   12

The interview itself   16

Someone else's interview   17

Work for your tutor   19

Extract from 'Wordpower' by R Lewis, p 11, National Extension College, 1977

Learners often need to be helped to make use of objectives, in whatever way they are phrased. Helped not just in a once-and-for-all way, by a list at the start of the text, but throughout the whole package. Objectives should appear as a natural ingredient of the learning material, linked closely with the text: eg, 'I'll pave the way to achieving objective 5 by saying a little about...'; and with self-assessment questions: 'This SAQ will show you how well you are meeting the main objective of this section'.

C | Checklist
What form of objectives do you need in order to communicate

— between yourselves
— to learners?

Objectives
On completion of the work in this unit you will be able to -

1. identify the main points to be considered when planning a course.
2. recognise inadequacies in a course proposal.
3. identify areas in a course proposal which need to be questioned and expanded.
4. design a course using the edtech approach.
   (After you have worked through this unit, I hope you will be able to achieve this objective. However I have not tackled it directly - except by the series of activities within the unit.)

Objectives as used by Dundee College of Education Diploma in Educational Technology (see 'Open Learning in Action', Volume 1 in this series, for an account of this course). Extract from 'Learning Resources in Diploma in Educational Technology Course Design' by G Manwaring, 2nd ed, p 2, Dundee College of Education, 1983

— I find the list of objectives at the beginning of a unit clears my mind and helps me to concentrate.
— I use the objectives as a summary when I have finished the unit — they give me what the unit has covered.
— I read through the objectives, work through the unit and then return to the objectives to tick off each one as it is achieved.

Objectives: learners comment on their usefulness

ENSURING A RANGE AND VARIETY OF OBJECTIVES
Most courses require learners to cover a range of different objectives. You need to check that your objectives succeed in this. Learners will often, for example, need to

— acquire knowledge and use it
— acquire skills and practise them
— develop particular attitudes.

Or, to put it another way, they will need to think, do and feel. The particular mix of these kinds of objectives will vary according to the course.

Kind of objective	Comment
Thinking	The processing of knowledge: it is the most widely used of the three, especially important in academic learning.
Doing	The development of physical skills, eg, manipulation: it plays a major role in training for certain trades, eg, brick-layer; in the past this kind of learning was accorded a lower status than the thinking kind.
Feeling	The development of feelings, attitudes, emotional responses: it is present in all learning, but is often ignored, perhaps because it is difficult to write objectives to facilitate this kind of learning. Attitudes are of crucial importance for some courses, eg, those training youth leaders, social-workers or counsellors.

But most learning involves more than one kind of objective; for example, the training of a doctor includes all three.

Kind of objective	Example
Thinking	Deciding which medicine to prescribe; recognizing a symptom.
Doing	Taking a pulse; stitching a wound.
Feeling	Communicating with patients of all ages and types.

The next table sets out various objectives. If you want to 'test yourself', cover the right-hand column and decide which of the three types is *most* involved in each case. Assume that each objective is prefaced by the words 'the learner should be able to'.

Objective	Kind of objective
Construct a working model of a steam engine, given the parts and necessary tools.	Doing (also thinking)
Justify the allocation of kidney machines to five particular individuals from a pool of ten for whom case histories are provided.	Thinking — at a high level (decision-making, evaluation)
Consult the local small-business service when next meeting a marketing problem.	Feeling (*willingness* to use a service, once informed of its existence)
Replace the fuse in an electric plug.	Doing
Join the local branch of the National Trust and take part in at least 30 per cent of its meetings in the first year of membership.	Feeling, showing commitment

As you'll have seen, the types of objective are not easily separable. Feelings are always involved to the extent that the learner must at least be willing to learn, and thinking will often be necessary even in skills development.

In spite of the importance of all three types most planners and writers over-use knowledge/thinking objectives, and even then concentrate only on the lower levels. These objectives are easier to write but they can lead to trivial, dull and irrelevant courses. So make sure that your list of objectives covers a wide enough range of capacities.

C **Checklist**

Which of the above types of objectives is or are most important for your own course?

Have you covered a wide enough range of objectives?

Have you paid enough attention to the development of attitudes, feelings and skills as well as knowledge?

Objectives also need to be varied in the level of challenge they make on the learner. As I mentioned above it is all too easy to concentrate only on the lower levels of objectives — they are after all often the easiest to write! The more demanding skills and capacities should be developed as well, as in the following examples from an O-level course.

Complexity	Example: History, World War I
Simple ↓ Complex	List the major battles of World War I. Classify the battles according to (a) numbers killed (b) geographical location. Choose the battle which you consider to have been the most important strategically and justify your choice.

The form in which the outcome is to be expressed can also be more or less demanding.

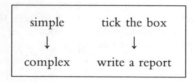

This is considered at greater length in the section on self-assessment.

C

Checklist

Take your list of objectives and see how well they stand up to the following questions. Revise any that seem unsatisfactory but remember that you are seeking workable rather than perfect objectives. You can always go back to modify the objectives after you have drafted some of your text.

Does each objective begin with a verb?

Is the learning outcome described exactly enough?

Is the learning outcome significant and relevant?

Does each objective describe one outcome only?

Does each objective respect the expertise and experience of the learner?

Is each objective attainable and realistic?

Are the objectives grouped in manageable ways? In particular, have you avoided over-long lists of objectives?

Is each objective clearly phrased?

Are your objectives phrased appropriately to the target audience?

Does each objective lead easily to a related assessment item? (See Section 2 of this book.)

Are your objectives written consistently to whatever format has been chosen?

Are your objectives varied in range and complexity?

Have you shown your objectives to other people for comment?

You may also like to refer to Appendix 1 which summarizes the qualities of a sound objective.

Quiz

1. One of the following statements is false. Which is it?

(a) Objectives are statements of learning outcomes.
(b) Objectives need a well-chosen verb.
(c) In a good course all outcomes will be planned.
(d) Objectives should describe learning that is desirable, observable and important.

2. Each of the following objectives is in one way or another inadequate. Can you say what is wrong with each one?

(a) I shall deal with three reasons.
(b) You should appreciate why this is an important topic.
(c) You will be able to define three major terms, use each in a sentence and apply each to your own work.

3. When writing objectives you will always need to include

— behaviour
— conditions
— standards.

Is this true or false?

4. Match the following two lists.

Person	Benefit of objectives
(a) writers	(i) help to advise potential learners
(b) learners	(ii) assist course planning and production
(c) counsellors	(iii) help to see whether appropriate to own needs
	(iv) help decide whether to send employees on a course

5. Once the course team has set the objectives these must then stand through the course production. Do you agree with this? Give a reason.

Answers

1. (c) is the odd one out. Unfortunately (perhaps?) it is not possible to spell out in advance every outcome. Some will be unexpected — for better or worse! This is not to underestimate the need for planning — at least *some* outcomes can be planned. (a), (b) and (d) are all correct and are discussed in the text.

2. You may have found other weaknesses but the ones I had in mind were:
(a) This is not expressed in terms of learner outcome. It describes the intention of the writer.
(b) The verb is not precise. 'Appreciate' refers to a state of mind rather than to recognizable behaviour.
(c) There are three objectives here. By running them all together the writer risks the learner missing one or two.

You really need to know the context of each objective but I hope that you have found this a useful exercise.

3. False. This is only one format for writing objectives. It would be used only if appropriate.

4. (a) and (ii): Objectives help writers to communicate with one another, to understand what each is doing.
(b) and (iii): Objectives help learners to assess whether a course, or part of it, is relevant.
(c) and (i): Objectives help counsellors and advisers when discussing the suitability of a course to a particular learner's needs.

(iv) is unpaired. If the first column had an entry 'employer', this would then be matched. An employer can look at the objectives of a course and decide whether it is relevant to his and his employees' needs.

5. Some direction is necessary but this statement, as it stands, is too inflexible. Objectives may be changed, for very good reasons, during the drafting process. Another reason for disagreeing is that objectives may have to be rephrased to make sense to learners. On the other hand, objectives can sometimes be changed for inadequate reasons, eg, to accommodate a senior course team member's particular specialism or because certain objectives are hard to teach.

Section Two. How to Write Self-Assessment Questions and Activities

How to write self-assessment questions and activities

CONTENTS
Introduction
The importance of self-assessment questions and activities
Writing self-assessment questions
Different types of self-assessment questions
Writing the activities

This section stresses the importance of self-assessment questions and activities to an open-learning package. They provide equivalents to the support offered to learners in a well run conventional class. Ten guidelines are suggested for writing questions. Different types of questions are illustrated to help you to vary your approach. The final section discusses the difference between a self-assessment question and an activity; it gives advice on how to write activities and use them in your course.

Activities, checklists and quizzes come at appropriate points in the text.

By working through this section you should be able to

— explain where self-assessment questions and activities come in the suggested sequence for writing an open-learning package
— decide what purposes self-assessment questions and activities will play in your course
— write effective self-assessment questions and activities together with feedback for them.

INTRODUCTION

First, a reminder of where you have got to in the suggested writing sequence. You have written the objectives. Now you write the assessment questions and activities that enable learners to check their progress to reaching the objectives. Only after questions and feedback have been written do you move on to preparing the linking text.

Self-assessment is a curiously neglected concept in much educational writing and practice. Not surprisingly, the learner often needs considerable help in becoming his own assessor. Yet this capacity is a vital part of becoming an autonomous learner and it can be fostered by careful design of the package. To master the skill of writing good self-assessment questions and activities is to go a long way to preparing successful learning materials. The provision of such questions together with the responses to them is the most obvious distinguishing feature of a package designed for use in open learning. In print form it leads to the open appearance of a page, with blocks of prose broken up by questions

29

and responses. But the principles outlined in this section hold good, whatever medium is chosen for the presentation of the learning material.

THE IMPORTANCE OF SELF–ASSESSMENT QUESTIONS AND ACTIVITIES

In a well run conventional class the following will occur:

— the tutor will ask questions that arouse the interest of the learners
— the learners will themselves have the chance to formulate questions to put to the tutor
— tutor and learners will talk to and with each other
— the tutor will give the learners the chance to test their own developing understanding and mastery of the objectives
— the tutor will guide the learners and provide feedback; such informal assessment can occur quite easily in a well run conventional class.

The situation for the open learner is more difficult. He may rarely, or even never, attend a class; he will be learning mainly on his own, in isolation from a teacher and from fellow-learners. He will have to elicit information on his own progress directly; he cannot rely on any tutor other than the package itself to indicate to him how well he is doing.

The challenge to the writer of open-learning materials is to provide in the package as many as possible of the above characteristics of a successful conventional class. This is what is meant by saying that an open-learning text should be interactive. With skill and imagination the writer can:

— ask questions that arouse the interest of the learners and prepare them for the study of a particular topic

---

Charles Newbould has been made redundant. He wants to use his £10,000 redundancy payment to set up a grocery business.
What issues does he need to consider?

FOR YOU   <u>Keywords</u>
TO DO
             1. Do you think of different things when you
                 see the following terms?

                 - Community Service
                 - Community involvement
                 - Community Action

             2. What kind of activities do you think young
                 people would be doing in a project which
                 calls itself:

                 - A community service project

                 - A community action project

                 - A community involvement project

             As you read through this item you should bear in
             mind any differences and similarities you have
             noted and see whether they are supported by the
             argument made here.

*Extract from the YMCA Certificate in Youth and Community Work. Workpack 1.
Evaluation p 2/4. Published by the YMCA National College*

— include questions and discussions of answers in the text to give the effect of a dialogue

---

```
FOR YOU      Think back over the last couple of weeks and
TO DO        list the number of occasions you yourself have
             received praise or recognition in your work.
```



```
Was the list you put together there very long?  Youth and
Community work, because of its very nature perhaps doesn't
receive its fair share of praise and recognition.  Our
managers often don't know exactly what we are doing in our
day to day work and so have to go on things like reports, the
way we present things at meetings and the gossip they hear,
to make any assessment of what we are doing.  The people we
are working with are frequently not in a position to know
what we do and whether it should be praised or recognised.
This often means that the main people who are in a position
to give us this sort of support are our colleagues. The
question then becomes do we make enough time in our work to
support other workers in this respect?  For ourselves one of
the most important sources for praise and recognition is
supervision.  Did that figure on your list?
```

Extract from the YMCA Certificate in Youth and Community Work. Workpack 2/6, sample learning materials, p 11. Published by the YMCA National College

— provide questions which give the learners the chance to check for themselves how well they are meeting course objectives

SAQ 4————————————————————————————

Go back over the previous section. Four advantages are given of using a strict format for your reports. List them briefly (one line to each).

Extract from 'Report Writing' by R Lewis and J Inglis, p 13, NEC, 1982

— provide feedback in the form of answers and discussion (in the absence of a tutor the answer or discussion provides the learner with the necessary comment on his attempt)

> It helps busy readers to find what they want
> It helps the writer to stay relevant
> It helps the writer to produce more effective written work — in whatever form
> It is good mental training.

Extract from 'Report Writing' by R Lewis and J Inglis, p 13, National Extension College, 1982. Answer to the previous self-assessment question

— include activities that enable learners to try out their new skills and understanding in the real world.

Optional Activity 10

If you can, add to your work any examples *you* have been able to find of particularly good or bad instructions.

Extract from 'Wordpower' by R Lewis, p 53, National Extension College, 1977

This last point is very important. Only by doing, by committing himself, can the learner be sure that he has learned something, or what it is that he still needs to work at.

Questions may be simple, or more complex.

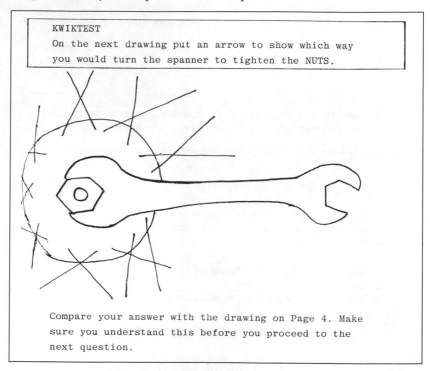

Cycle maintenance for nine-year-olds. Produced at a writers' workshop

```
    Marx said that Religion is the opium of the masses.
    Do you feel he was attacking religion, the naivity
    of the people or both.

    Circle your answer:

        ┌─────────────────────────────┐
        │ Religion                     │
        │                       Both   │
        │ The People                   │
        └─────────────────────────────┘

    The simple phrase is more complex than it appears and
    to answer that question we need really to go back to the
    context in which the quotation is used ........
```

Extract from 'How to Write Self-Assessment Questions' by Nigel Paine, p 7, SCET Open Learning Paper No. 402

It is sometimes said that open learners are at a disadvantage compared with learners in more conventional classes. But in some ways they are actually better placed. They have time to think about the questions and to consider their answers. If they wish, they can draft their answer several times. In class they must answer 'on the spot'. The course writer similarly has time to consider, prepare and test out his questions and to assemble responses not only from his colleagues but also from learners, collected during the process of piloting the package. He can thus work on the phrasing of his questions until they are unambiguous and can offer alternative answers and additional points.

Case-study
The case-study of Clwyd A-level sociology in *Open Learning in Action* (CET, 1984) has a discussion of the importance of self-assessment questions in that scheme.

Activity
Select which of the following functions you will want self-assessment questions or activities to carry out in your own course:

— rousing the interest of the learners
— encouraging the learners to generate their own questions
— setting up a dialogue
— enabling learners to check their own developing skill and understanding.

Consider the kinds of questions you might ask. Make some rough notes before reading on. The next part of this section will help you to refine your questions.

WRITING SELF-ASSESSMENT QUESTIONS
So how do you set about writing self-assessment questions (from now on I shall call these SAQs), whether these are of the preparatory sort (motivating the learner for what is to come, bringing to the surface his existing knowledge) or those which are retrospective (enabling the learner to check whether or not, and what, he has learned from a particular section of your package)? This section offers ten guidelines to help you to draft effective questions.

1. The SAQ should relate to course objectives
If the objective has been adequately developed then the assessment question will follow logically.

Objective	The learner will be able to lay out a simple business letter.
SAQ 1	The following are a number of examples of letter openings. Which one is laid out correctly? [Examples would be displayed here.]
SAQ 2	Label the various features of the correct example.
SAQ 3	Take the faulty layouts and lay each one out in the correct order.

2. All objectives should be tested, preferably more than once

A common practice, adopted for example in the Pan self-study series 'Breakthrough to Business' and in the AnCO marketing modules, is to test each objective twice, once in the text and once at the end of a unit, chapter or section. In text the questions may be called 'Self checks' and, at the end of a section, 'Check your learning' or 'Review questions' or some other similar term. The two questions should be different, to make the learner think and to add variety. For example, if the objective is to list the sources of information necessary to write a report, the text can say:

'After you have worked through this chapter you should be able to

— list possible sources of the information necessary to write a report'.

Below is an example of an in-text question.

SAQ 1

Look back at the examples given in the last unit — the Thorn 450K, the typing chairs, the college of further education, the hotel. (a) What kinds of information were used in each case? (You will find one or two under each.) (b) Add any further kinds you can think of which the report writer might have consulted, in each column. Some examples have been given to start you off.

Extract from 'Report Writing' by R Lewis and J Inglis, p 29, National Extension College, 1982

Next is an example of an end-of-chapter question.

CHECK YOUR LEARNING

1. In the previous chapter we gave terms of reference for a report as follows:

> To a Works Foreman . . . 'We seem to be experiencing problems because of poor communication between the Machine Shop and the Chief Engineer. Please look into this and submit a report to the Plant Manager.'

Would you say that the information for this report would be gained

   (a) mainly through personal contact and discussions
   (b) though reading printed material
   (c) from objects in the factory?

Extract from 'Report Writing' by R Lewis and J Inglis, p 36, National Extension College, 1982

3. The questions should be inviting to the learner

He should feel that it is worthwhile answering them. They should be interesting, even intriguing, and they should be relevant. Sometimes it will also be necessary to encourage the learner a little.

```
If you want to see how much you have learned, try

this ...


Five minutes on the next question will save an

hour later.
```

Extract produced at a writers' workshop, 1983

4. Questions should be realistic in the demands they make

You should always choose the quickest and most direct way of testing understanding. SAQs requiring long answers are likely to be ignored by learners. It is often possible to split a long question up into several short ones. It is also often possible to test quite complex objectives by questions set out simply.

> According to the text, which of the following best
> distinguishes poetry from prose?
>
> (a) line length
> (b) rhyme
> (c) imagery
> (d) symbolism
>
> Write a sentence to justify your choice.

Extract produced at a writers' workshop, 1983

SAQ 2: *Which of the following commodities can be produced using just* land *and* labour?

bread	fruit	furniture
haircuts	books	aircraft

SAQ 2:   None of them can! Bread requires bakery ovens, delivery vans and shops; fruit needs (at the very least) baskets for gathering; furniture needs hammers, saws, screwdrivers and glue-pots; haircuts need scissors, and so on. As I go on to explain in the text, very little can be produced without capital.

Extract from 'Economics "A" level' by Adrian Perry, Volume 1, pp 6, 14, National Extension College, 1983

5. Questions should be varied in type and in the length of answer required
The next section considers variety in the formats of SAQs.

6. Questions should be frequent
Questions should appear, say, one to 750 words, or one to a page — whatever is thought appropriate to the target audience. An SAQ should always be in sight.

7. Questions should make clear to the learner exactly what is required
They should be clearly structured and clearly written in an appropriate tone (see p 39 for example).

8. The writer should provide any study advice necessary to help the learner to answer
See p 40 for example.

Instead of:

> There have been countless inventions which have changed our lives during the C20th: TV, radio, telephone, motorcar and X-ray are a few obvious ones but there are many more.

You could have:

> There have been countless inventions which have changed our lives during the C20th. Jot down the ones that spring immediately to mind:
>
> > Inventions:
>
> You probably wrote down, the motorcar, TV and radio, X-ray and the telephone.

But it would have been more structured and less ambiguous if you had made the demands on the student quite specific:

> There have been countless inventions which have changed our lives during the C20th. Jot down three or four as they spring to mind. Do not spend more than 30 seconds on this.
>
> Inventions:
> 1.   2.
> 3.   4.
>
> My list was fairly long, but the first four or five I put down were: the motorcar, TV and radio, the telephone and X-rays. Of course the aeroplane, the computer, satellites and space travel are others you may have had. You may well have thought of others too.

Extract from 'How to Write Self–Assessment Questions' by Nigel Paine, pp 5, 6, SCET Open Learning Paper No. 402

Turn to p 38 and answer the questions there.	curt; no advice or help given on how to answer
To check that you've grasped this important point, turn to p 38. Read the questions carefully before answer ing.Then write about two sentences for each answer. This should take you about 15 minutes.	some persuasion given to answer the question a friendly tone advice on how to set about the task

9. Questions should be signposted visually and in accordance with an agreed convention

The learner should immediately see that a question is coming up. Symbols or 'flags' are often useful — you have met some of these already such as the question mark and tick. Any symbols or verbal identifiers (such as 'self check' or 'quiz' should be used consistently throughout and the conventions should be clearly explained when they first appear.

What are 'SAQs'?

You are working on a self-study course – this is different from a textbook in that it expects you to stop and carry out work at certain points. You learn by doing and doing in this case usually means *writing*. If this is the first time that you have studied with NEC then you might be surprised to find the pages broken up with what we call 'SAQs' (self-assessment questions). For these we use this symbol: [?] We ask you a question, you write down your answer and then you move on to read what we have to say. You compare your answer with ours.

It is very important to write your own answer down first; that is the way to learn. You'll find that our answers will nearly always be longer than yours. Don't worry about this. We have to answer very fully to take account of what *many* students might say. Also, we have been able to put more time into our answer than you have. And you are studying this course to learn something; if you could answer all the questions fully right from the start then there would be no point in becoming a student! So:

- answer all the SAQs by writing briefly in a notebook. Don't read our answer. (You could use a piece of card to hide these and remove temptation!)
- *Then* read our answers. Don't be put off by the length of the answers we give.

Extract from 'Preparing for Social Science' by L Maynard and R Lewis, p 18, National Extension College, 1981

10. Questions should be followed by an answer, or response

This is one open-learning equivalent of the tutor's response in the classroom. Ideally answers to SAQs should take into account a wide range of likely learner answers and level of response. The writer should show how the correct answer is arrived at and offer guidance to the learner who may have made a mistake. Where necessary reference should be made to other parts of the course or to follow-up work, eg, for the unsure or very advanced learner.

Answers to SAQ 25:

   (a) 1911   73.6 − men
                   76.7 − women
                  150.3

       1911 average = 75.15 (Total − 150.3; divided by 2 (men + women))

If you got (a) wrong then go back to SAQ 25 and work through the optional loop before returning to recalculate the figures for 1951 and 1971.

Extract from 'Preparing for Social Science' by L Maynard and R Lewis, p 90, National Extension College, 1981

Responses should be of an appropriate length. For a quick self-check question, for example, the response could be a word or two together with a reference to the preceding text; for a longer, more open-ended question the discussion may be extended.

The feedback, whether it be headed 'answer', 'discussion' or 'response', should be put in an appropriate place. Where this is will depend upon the subject matter, the kind of question asked, and the learner. Sometimes answers will need to be concealed, at other times easily accessible. Questions intended to alert the learner to what is coming next may be followed by a line or other 'pause' symbol. To have to turn over several pages or turn the book upside down would in this case be disruptive and unnecessary. But if the learner is checking his progress after having completed a section of the text then there is a case for concealing the answers, eg, by placing them at the end of the book (maybe on coloured paper) or on the next page or upside down. Whatever policy is adopted it should be explained to the learner, who needs to know where to find the answers — and it must be consistently applied.

If the answers are grouped together then there is an obvious danger that the learner's eye will stray to the answer to the next question. One very clever but simple way of preventing this is to put the *answers* in numerical sequence but the number of SAQs in the text in another sequence (eg, 3,5,1,6,2,4). Thus, when the student reads the answer to SAQ 1 he will not easily locate the answer to the next question he will be asked.

But you might ask, 'What if the learner ignores the SAQs or cheats by reading the answers before working out his own? There are two responses to this, one more positive than the other. The first is to say that in providing the questions at least you've done *your* best; if the learner chooses to ignore them that's his decision. The other response is more positive. People learn in a whole variety of ways, we each have our own preferred learning style. Thus the package will be, and should be, adapted by each individual to suit his own way of learning. Some learners will tackle each and every question; others will try some in detail, maybe those questions they feel unsure of, and miss others out. The learner may commit his answers to paper or answer 'in his head'; responses given in the text may be read carefully or ignored. How have *you* been using the quizzes, activities and checklists in this book? Would you say that the method you have chosen is 'right' or 'wrong'?

Activity
Write some SAQs together with feedback to them. Then check your SAQs against the following questions. Modify your SAQs and answers as necessary.

Checklist
Writing SAQs
Does each SAQ relate to an objective of your course?

Have you tested each and every objective? Once or twice?

Are your SAQs attractive? Will the learner want to answer them?

Is it clear how each SAQ will help the learner?

Are your SAQs realistic? Will the learner be able to answer them?

Have you divided long and complex questions into shorter and simpler ones?

Are your SAQs varied in type? (See next section, together with checklist)

Are your SAQs varied in length and nature of answer/outcome?

Is the learner given a clear instruction of the length and type of answer expected?

Are your SAQs frequent enough? Is an SAQ always in sight?

Are your SAQs clearly constructed?

Are your SAQs written in clear language? Are there any difficult words that might be unfamiliar to the learner?

Have you provided any study advice necessary to help the learner to answer?

Do your SAQs clearly stand out? Have you used a symbol or other convention to identify them?

Writing answers to SAQs
Have you provided an answer or response to each SAQ?

Are your answers clear?

Have you reinforced the correct answer?

Have you given guidance on wrong answers?

Have you explained how the correct answer is arrived at?

Have you referred to other parts of the course?

Have you set follow-up work?

Are your responses of an appropriate length?

Are your responses in an appropriate place?

Have you considered the learners' feelings — eg, congratulated learners on correct answers; sympathized with learners who make mistakes that are common?

(NB. Not every question will apply to every case. Select, and attend to, those which are relevant to you.)

You can refine your questions a good deal by using this checklist; as with objectives, you must be prepared to draft and redraft till you get the questions and responses right. But you should also pilot your questions in draft, ie, try them out on learners: using even only two or three learners can give you very useful feedback. You or a colleague can watch learners while they use the text. You can ask them, directly or by questionnaire, whether they experienced any difficulties with the questions and how long they took. Their answers to the questions in the package can also be collected and used in the finished product. This gives an air of interest and reality to the text; learners enjoy seeing the work of their peers in print.

Activity
Pilot your questions in draft. Revise your questions in the light of comments.

DIFFERENT TYPES OF SAQ
This section shows the range of SAQs that writers can use. If you are aware of the possibilities then it is more likely that you will vary the SAQs you set and thus retain the learners' interest. There are two main categories of question:

— those where everything is given
— those where the learner is asked to provide some information himself.

In the former the learner has to select the correct response from those given. Examples are:

— multiple-choice questions, eg, choose one option; choose more than one option
— variants of multiple-choice questions, eg, true/false and matching lists
— sequencing, eg, placing a list of items in order of importance or size
— completing sentences, using words or symbols provided.

In the latter, the learner has to introduce some new information or place information in a new form. The outcome may be short — a word, a list, a phrase, a sentence — or more extended — a paragraph, a plan, an essay, a report.

Questions where all the information is provided
The multiple-choice question (MCQ)
The most powerful kind of question is the multiple-choice question. This is made up of a 'stem' followed by a series of possible answers ('options'). One of these is correct (the 'key') and the others are 'distractors'. They should all be plausible and perfectly built around mistakes learners often make.

```
    According to the text, which of the following best
distinguishes poetry from prose?

(a) line length

(b) rhyme

(c) imagery

(d) symbolism
```

Extract produced at a writers' workshop, 1983

```
    A control group

(a) is a comparable group tested in a different experiment
(b) refers to the people running one experiment
(c) does not receive the variable being studied
(d) none of the above
```

Extract from the YMCA Certificate in Youth and Community Work. Workpack 2. Induction module, p WP2/6

Unfortunately, this is rarely used in open-learning packages because it takes longer to construct than other kinds of question. Writers may be intimidated because they know that, when used for formal assessment, this is a complex question to produce. But there is a difference between writing MCQs for use in formal assessment and using them for informal self-assessment. The procedures needed for the former are very rigorous; of the many questions tested only a few are retained to be entered into the question bank. MCQs used to further learning are in many ways easier and much more under the control of the writer, who can provide answers and discuss these with the learner.

If you are writing MCQs for informal self-assessment then you can break the rules, for example by including more than one 'right' answer if this suits your teaching purposes, as in the following.

Tick which of the following statements are true. (You can tick more than one.)

Multiple-choice questions:

☐   are relatively quick to answer

☐   require the learner to select one or more alternatives from a list

☐   require the learner to recall rather than to recognize an answer

☐   require the learner to formulate an extended answer

(The last two answers are false.)

Remember the advice given in the previous section: provide a full response to the learners and comment on *all* possible choices. Deal especially with common misconceptions.

Here, for example, are the responses provided for the two questions on page 44.

```
(a) Good. Well done. Unit --- (page ---) explains why
this is the most obvious distinguishing feature of
poetry.

If your response was (b), (c) or (d) then you have not
picked up the point made in the unit about the most
reliable distinguishing feature. Many poems do rhyme
but some do not. Similarly, many poems use imagery and
many use symbols but it would be easy to find exceptions
in each case. The unit argues that line length is
nearly always significant.
```

Extract produced at a writers' workshop, 1983

```
Answer C

(NB.  This example could be improved by extending the answer, eg,
to reinforce the correct response and to discuss responses a, b
and d.)
```

*Extract from the YMCA Certificate in Youth and Community Work. Workpack 2.
Induction Module, p WP2/6*

Many people think that MCQs are suitable only for scientific and technical
subjects. They have, however, been successfully used in a variety of subjects
including keep fit and business studies. Appendix 3 gives more hints on how
to write MCQs.

Matching lists

This is a related type of question. The learner is presented with two lists of
data and he has to match them.

```
Place in the box following each statement (1-3) the
letter corresponding to the heat transfer process
involved (A-D).

1.   The handle of a poker placed on a fire becomes hot. ☐

2.   Bread can be toasted in front of a fire. ☐

3.   A fire warms a room. ☐


A.   Radiation
B.   Radiation and convection
C.   Radiation, convection and conduction
D.   Conduction
```

Extract produced at a writers' workshop, 1983

True/false questions

These ask the learner to indicate which of the list of statements is true and
which false. This is done most simply by putting a T/F at the end of each
statement.

Before we look at the other rooms in your home let's consider some of the things people say about saving energy:

1. Keeping the immersion heater on all day is cheaper than switching it on only when you need hot water. T/F

2. The best place for a radiator is under the window. T/F

3. Drawing thick curtains at dusk saves almost as much heat as double-glazing. T/F

Extract produced at a writers' workshop, 1983

Since the learner has a 50 per cent chance of getting the right answer it is as well not to use this type of question too frequently. As always, the discussion that follows is important to consolidate learning.

Answer

(a) False, because you are not taking advantage of cheap tariffs.

(b) False, as you will be heating up the coldest air in the room - the air that is coming in from outside. But if you have good double-glazing it is just as cheap to have the radiator under the window as anywhere else in the room.

(c) True. After sunset the outside temperature lowers dramatically. The thick curtains will act as a form of insulation.

Extract produced at a writers' workshop, 1983

Another type of question provides a list of points and asks the learner to put these in order according to a criterion, eg, in terms of importance or sequence.

CHECK YOUR LEARNING

1. In longer reports it is possible that many different sections may be used. Put the following sections into the order in which you would expect them to appear in such reports:

   Conclusion — Title page — Appendix — Main body — Recommendations — Contents page — Introduction

Extract from 'Report Writing' by R Lewis, p 84, National Extension College, 1982

The response section should list the correct sequence and draw the learner's attention to particular points of interest.

Another kind of SAQ requires the learner to fill blank spaces by selecting appropriate words or phrases.

```
The assumption of facts because they conform to patterns
from the past is called .........

.............. is the study of the past.

When we look at the way the past has been studied this
is known as .....

Fill in the missing words from the following list:

history
histiography
historicism
```

There are problems with this kind of question. If used frequently it can quickly become routine and dull. It can sometimes also be easy for a learner to get the correct answer without really understanding, eg, by using grammatical clues or because only one word is left.

There are ways of getting round some of these problems, eg, by providing more words than there are blank spaces.

```
When devising SAQs, (a) _____ type questions are
most suitable for linking facts and dates while (b)
_____ type questions are more appropriate for
assembling equipment.

Fill in the blanks choosing the missing words from the
list below:

- mutiple-choice
- matching lists
- sequencing
- completing blanks.
```

(a) Matching lists (b) Sequencing

The previous section explained that matching list
questions were particularly useful when two sets of
data were involved and that sequencing questions helped
when the order of operations was important.   It would
be possible to use the other two types and, eg, to test
assembling equipment by a series of multiple-choice
questions.   But would this be as economical and effective?

So far in this section I have considered questions which provide the learner
with all the necessary information and which require him to select an answer
or manipulate the information in some way, eg, by sequencing it. Such
questions are particularly useful for self-assessment purposes since they can be
quickly and easily answered.

Questions where the learner has to provide some information himself
Questions requiring the learner to construct a response take several forms. At
the simplest, you can ask the learner to produce one word, perhaps by filling
in a blank. Or, more ambitiously...

There are many different sorts of produce which may be
marketed by cooperative.   You will find four types of
produce listed on p 33.

- Can you think of any other types of produce not listed
here?

- What produce do farmers in your area sell?

Or you can ask for a list (as in SAQ 4, *Report Writing*, see overleaf). In some
courses an objective is that the learner should be able to write fluently. In this
case it is appropriate to ask for longer responses.

SAQ 4_____

Write up the section on Office Practice into one paragraph using some or all of the information given in the office-practice column. Write straightforward sentences. Don't forget to start with a clear topic sentence.

You should have something like this:

> Office Practice is a very varied subject. It has areas of overlap with Business English. You have to learn how to set up and operate a filing system in the office and to be able to use the many machines that you would expect to find in an office. We have plain-paper copiers which can produce about five copies every second, and we have to be able to type stencils and operate a duplicator.

All of the paragraph is concerned with Office Practice, though it is perhaps not as fluent as it might be. The topic sentence stresses how varied the subject is and some details from the column (e.g. its difficulty) are omitted. It is at this stage in report writing that you will usually find you can discard some of the information you have collected, for reasons of space or relevance, or to communicate more clearly with your reader.

Extract from 'Report Writing' by R Lewis, p 62, National Extension College, 1982

Every possible help should be provided; notice in the above example the guidance on length (one paragraph), style (straightforward sentences) and method (start with a topic sentence).

It is possible to extend the level of challenge by asking for an essay plan or its equivalent (eg, the framework of a report). But it can be difficult to provide feedback in the text to cover all eventualities, and such questions are often more suitable for tutor–assessment (see Section 3).

Case studies are another useful kind of question. The learner is involved in an interesting case and a range of questions is then asked based on the information provided. There is an example on p 51.

Another useful kind of question asks the learner to complete or to label a drawing, graph or diagram. Or to identify labels A, B, C, etc, on a diagram — maybe selecting from a list of given words.
Examples are given on pp 52 and 53.

Incidentally the SAQ answer here would be improved by adding a sentence or two to the effect 'Make sure you didn't connect Box (x) to Box (y). This is a common mistake. Did you?'

Looking at maps_____

Often we only need maps to tell us where roads go — to plan a journey, say, or what to see. And we use maps which have distances already filled in, like this

But for more detail, it's best to use Ordnance Survey (OS) maps.

Scale 1 to 25,000   Sheet SK 64

This shows part of Sheet SK64, near Nottingham.
The scale is 1 to 25 000 — good for walkers, as footpaths and hedges are shown.

1 1 cm represents 25 000 cm on the ground. What is this in metres?

2 How many cm stand for 1 kilometre?

3 Use a ruler to find the distance along the footpath from Gunthorpe to Caythorpe over the Car Dyke.

4 Find the length of the footpath circuit running Gunthorpe — Caythorpe — road — back along towing path.

5 How long would you take to walk it? (Assume you can walk at 4 km per hour)

6 How long is the road leading to Glebe Farm?

7 If you left Gunthorpe school at 2.30 pm, when would you expect to reach Trentside Cottage following the circuit of question (4).

8 How wide is the River Trent at this point?

9 The straight lines mark off kilometres. How far apart would they be on a map with a scale of 1 to 50 000?

10 Roughly how far is it from the Footpath end (A) to the School in Gunthorpe?

Now change these map measurements into full-size ones:

11 6 mm, scale 1 to 25 000

12 13 mm, scale 1 to 50 000

13 24 mm, scale 1 to 10 000

And change these full-size measurements to map distances

14 150 m, scale 1 to 10 000

15 40 km, scale 1 to 50 000

16 Change 8 miles to kilometres by multiplying by 1.6, and find the map distance for a scale of 1 to 25 000.

Check answers at the back

Extract from 'Numbers at Work' by J Gillespie, p 78, National Extension College, 1980

SAQ   B.13

Label the boxes shown below and form a block diagram to show how a
two–way radio telephony link may be connected.

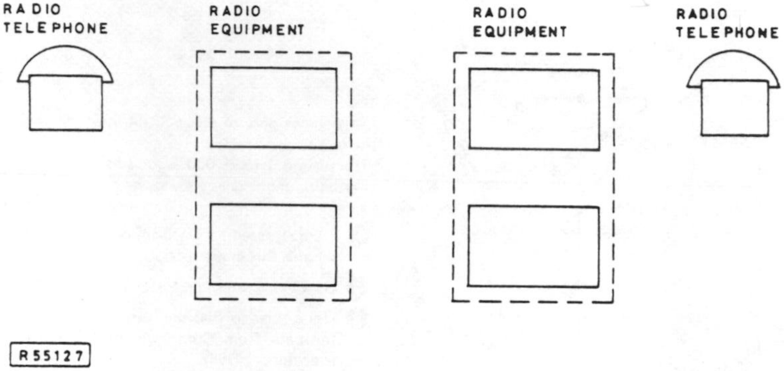

RADIO
TELEPHONE

RADIO
EQUIPMENT

RADIO
EQUIPMENT

RADIO
TELEPHONE

R 55127

Fig. B.40

SAQ   D.9

Form a primary radar system by connecting the blocks together that are
shown in Fig. D.19. Show also any arrow signs that may be appropriate.

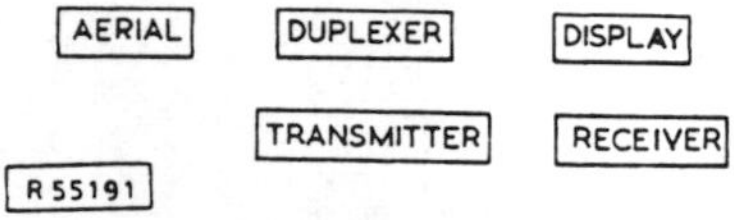

AERIAL   DUPLEXER   DISPLAY

TRANSMITTER   RECEIVER

R 55191

Fig. D.19

These examples are taken from Telecommunications Systems I. TEC U76.007

*Extract from 'How to Write a Distance-Learning Course. 5. Assessment' by
R Lewis, p 47, Council for Educational Technology, 1980, using British Telecom
'Telecommunications Systems 1 Tec U76.007'*

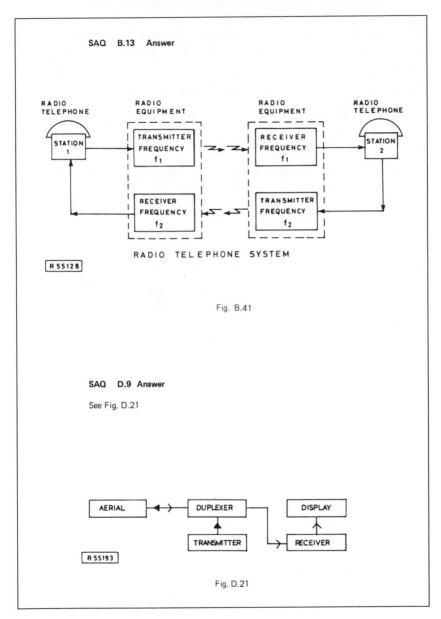

SAQ   B.13   Answer

RADIO TELEPHONE SYSTEM

R 5512B

Fig. B.41

SAQ   D.9   Answer

See Fig. D.21

R 55193

Fig. D.21

Extract from 'How to Write a Distance-Learning Course. 5. Assessment' by R Lewis, p 48, Council for Educational Technology, 1980, using British Telecom 'Telecommunications Systems 1 Tec U76.007'

Other SAQs

I have looked at two major subdivisions of SAQs: those where all the information is given and those requiring the learner to supply information himself. But the two categories are not totally separate one from the other. It's easy to combine elements from both, eg, to set a MCQ but also to ask the learner to give a reason for selecting the response, as in the poetry example on pages 44 and 45.

Sometimes SAQs require the learner to carry out practical operations such as using a calculator. In these cases the writer would refer to any necessary equipment and advise the learner on what to do in the event of meeting any difficulties.

The following are examples of practical SAQs.

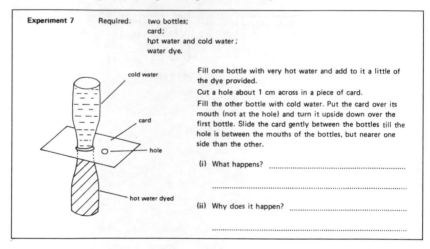

Experiment 7   Required: two bottles;
card;
hot water and cold water;
water dye.

Fill one bottle with very hot water and add to it a little of the dye provided.

Cut a hole about 1 cm across in a piece of card.

Fill the other bottle with cold water. Put the card over its mouth (not at the hole) and turn it upside down over the first bottle. Slide the card gently between the bottles till the hole is between the mouths of the bottles, but nearer one side than the other.

(i) What happens? ....

....

(ii) Why does it happen? ....

....

Answers to Experiment 7

(i) The coloured water rises in a stream up one side of the top bottle.

(ii) The water in the lower bottle is hot and is therefore lighter or less dense than the water in the upper bottle.

Theory

Hot water streams upwards through the hole; cold water runs down to replace it though this cannot easily be seen. In this way a convection current carrying hot water upwards and cold water downwards is set up.

The dye is only to show up the convection current in the water; it plays no part in causing the process.

Experiment design

The hole must not be too small; hot and cold water streams have to get through in opposite directions.

The bottom bottle must be absolutely full; an air bubble will stop the action.

Extensions

Would two holes help? One for hot water rising and one for cold returning?

How could you help the hot water to choose one hole only?

Does this have practical applications?

Extract from 'Laboratory Practical Units in Physical Science, Unit 8, Heat' by J L Patterson and D T Wilson, Dundee College of Education, 1977

```
Take a milk bottle, a wine bottle, and a jam jar.  Guess their volumes
in cubic centimetres, and jot down your 'guesstimates'.

Now fill each with cold water.  In turn empty each into a bowl on your
kitchen scales, weighing the water (in grams) in each case.  Now the
weight in grams of the water from each container equals the container's
volume in cubic centimetres.  Compare your 'guesstimates' with the true
results.  How near were you?



Response
You were probably surprised to find how much your 'guesstimates' are
influenced by the shape, not size of the containers!  If you guessed
within 20% in each case - splendid.  If not, don't worry, the ability
to guess volumes develops rapidly with practice - and now you know
one way of practising.
```

Examples written by Phil Race, National Extension College tutor

A

Activity

Practise writing different types of SAQ. Vary your format. Take one objective and find two or three different ways of testing it with SAQs. This will be time well spent as you will be

— building up your own bank of questions for use in your course
— developing your skill at writing this crucial part of an open-learning package.

Then check your work against the following checklist.

C

Checklist

Have you used a variety of types of question? Tick which of the following you have tried.

Those where everything is given	Those where the learner must supply an answer
MCQ	One word
Matching list	List
True/false	Phrase
Putting points in a sequence or hierarchy	Sentence
	Paragraph
Blank spaces with words, etc, provided from which the learners must select	Plan
	Case-study with questions
Drawing a graph	Drawing a graph
	Practical SAQ

Quiz

Q

1. Which of the following is the order for preparing a package recommended in the text?
(a) write SAQ answers; write text; write objectives; write questions
(b) write text; write objectives; write questions; write SAQ answers
(c) write questions; write objectives; write text; write SAQ answers
(d) write objectives; write questions; write SAQ answers; write text

2. Which of the following functions can be performed by an SAQ and its answer?
(a) arousing interest
(b) enabling the learner to check progress
(c) creating dialogue
(d) providing feedback

3. In which of the following places should answers to SAQs be placed?
(a) immediately below the question itself
(b) upside down on the same page
(c) at the back of the book

4. It is not worth piloting SAQs unless you can do this with a decent-sized group of learners, 50 at least. T/F?

5. One of the writers in your team consistently uses only one type of SAQ format — filling in the blanks. What might you say to him?

6. The following list of statements relates to MCQs when used for self-assessment. Two of the statements are true. Which are they?
(a) Only one answer can be right.
(b) Comment needs to be provided on each response.
(c) Incorrect responses should represent common misconceptions.
(d) MCQs are suitable only for scientific and technical subjects.

Answers
1. The sequence recommended in the text is (d). That's not to say that the others wouldn't work; there can be no 'right' way. But you were asked for the sequence recommended in this book and so (d) is the correct answer.

2. All these functions can be performed by SAQs. See the text for a discussion. You may, of course, disagree!

3. Another 'trick' question! There is no correct answer to this one, or rather all are correct. It all depends on your learners, your objectives and the subject matter. If you are using a medium other than print for your course then you will have to take different decisions about where to place your answers.

4. This is false, according to the text. You can get very useful feedback from even one learner.

5. You might choose to warn him of the limitations of this kind of question — it is possible on occasions to answer correctly without understanding. You might also stress the monotonous nature of encountering one kind of SAQ again and again. It turns learners off. You might recommend the writer to try out other SAQ formats, show him the work of other writers, produce samples — or take some other similar course of action.

6. (b) and (c) are the correct responses. (a) is not true. If you were writing MCQs for assessment then you would be bound by the rule of only one correct answer. But the text argues that you have flexibility on this, when writing for self-assessment. (d) is not true. MCQs can be used very successfully in a whole range of subjects, though some people still find this hard to believe.

WRITING THE ACTIVITIES

Self-assessment questions are usually limited in structure. You ask a question and feel confident that you can, within reason, anticipate likely responses. SAQs are, in fact, often carefully structured so that likely responses are kept within a certain range.

But sometimes your objective will not easily be tested in this way. You may not only want the learner to check his understanding but also his ability to try out a newly acquired skill or capacity in the real world. It may be of the essence that he goes and does something. One way of achieving this in an open-learning package is by setting activities. The last two SAQs given on pages 54 and 55 are steps towards this. Here are other examples.

ACTIVITY 1_____

If you have any friends or colleagues who write regularly, ask them how they set about the job of writing. Ask them what they think of the advice given in this book.

ACTIVITY 2_____

Try this sequence out when writing your reports. Or just try out one or two parts of it and see what difference this makes.

Extract from 'Report Writing' by R Lewis, p 77, National Extension College, 1982

---

on buying is the decision of the investor.

Activity

Try following the financial pages over the next week. Note any announcement (government policy, firm changes) and see how these affect share prices.

HOW LITTLE CAN I INVEST?
This can vary, and part of the variation can be due to inflation. Whilst the present figure is around £500, it is always wise to ask before getting involved.

Extract from 'Funding Your Future' by T Clarke, p 46, NEC, 1982

Look at your tongue in a mirror. Can you see any difference between the areas of the tongue?

Make up a glass of salt water and of sugary water, and one of vinegary water. Try dipping your finger in the salt water and then dropping a drop onto the front, back and sides of the tongue. (You may wash out your mouth after each drop.)

Where do you taste the salt?

Repeat with sugar and vinegar. Where are sweet and sour substances tasted?

Do the areas correspond to the areas marked out overleaf? (or on page 91, Becket)

Extract from 'Digestion — the Mouth' Unit AP5, Telford College of Further Education Department of Science and Applied Mathematics

agreements one party states that the agreement is 'binding in honour only' and in this case the legal intent has been specifically removed.

Activity

A football pool coupon is an agreement lacking this essential element of legal intent. Obtain a coupon and try to find the clause which is contained on all football pools which removes the legal intent. Think of the reason why football pools companies remove this.

Although it is assumed that in most agreements 'legal intent' is present unless specifically removed, in domestic and social arrangements the assumption is the opposite, i.e. the court will assume the absence of legal intent unless it is specifically included. Thus if a father promises his son an extra £1 a week for

Extract from 'Practical Business Law' by T Price (Pan Breakthrough Series) p 44, 1982

Practical 1:   To find the effect of forced breathing and exercise on the
ventilation rate

You will need either a stop watch, or watch with a second hand, and a notebook.

Work with a friend, one person "breathing" and one person timing, then change
over. If you feel at all faint during this experiment, then stop immediately.
It is not dangerous, but you should not carry this activity out if you suffer
from asthma, other respiratory diseases or heart disease.

1. Count the number of normal breaths the subject takes in 2 minutes.

    Number of breaths/min = _____

2. Now hold your breath for as long as possible, and take your partner's
    pulse.

    Breath held after "normal" breathing for _____/secs

                    Pulse rate = _____/sec

3. Allowing breathing to be as deep as possible, count breaths for a further
    2 minutes (maximum ventilation).

    Number of breaths/min = _____

4. Repeat No 2

5. Now run up and down 4 flights of stairs, run up and down on the spot for
    2 minutes or take similar sudden exercise. As soon as you have finished,
    take a deep breath and hold for as long as possible. Count your breaths
    for the next 2 minutes.

    Breath held for   = _____/secs

    Number of breaths   = _____/min

    Pulse rate   = _____

What comparisons can you make between these figures?

_____

_____

_____

How, in biological terms, could you explain them?

_____

_____

_____

Extract from Telford College of Further Education material

Case-study

CS The Zoo Animal Management case-study in Volume 1 of this series (*Open Learning in Action*, CET, 1984) has examples of activities used to train zookeepers.

Activities enable the learner to relate the standard package to his own unique individual experience. It may still be necessary for you to provide some kind of feedback on the likely results of an activity, though there probably won't be a 'correct' answer as there usually is with an SAQ.

It is also possible to mix activity and SAQ as in the example on p 60, which sets an activity and then moves in the last question to something more nearly resembling an SAQ, to which an answer could be provided.

Activity

A Decide whether your course would benefit from the inclusion of activities.

Settle on the function these activities would perform.

Write some activities.

Check them against the following list of questions.

Checklist

C Does your activity relate to an objective of your course?

Is your activity attractive? Will the learner want to try it?

Are the purposes of your activity clear?

Is your activity realistic in the demands it makes on the learner?

Have you structured your activity in such a way that the learners can tackle it?

Is the likely outcome of your activity indicated?

Have you given any necessary advice to the learners on how to carry out the activity?

Are your activities varied?

Have you used enough activities?

Do your activities clearly stand out in the package? Have you used a symbol or some other convention to identify them?

Have you borne any safety considerations in mind?

Have you referred your learner to further sources of help either inside or outside the package?

 Quiz
Can you give one difference between an SAQ and an activity?

Answers
Here are some possibilities.

SAQs are usually limited in structure; activities can be more wide-ranging.

SAQs are usually closed-ended, leading towards a right answer; activities are more open-ended.

SAQs usually test the learner's mastery of a particular section of text; activities turn the learner out to the world outside the package and ask him to use or apply his learning.

SAQs usually stay within the text; activities help the learner to relate the package to his own experience.

Section Three. Other Means of Helping Learners to Assess Their Progress

Other means of helping learners to assess their progress

CONTENTS
Self-help groups
A tutor
Face-to-face sessions
New technology

This section explores other ways that may be open for you to help learners assess their progress — self-help groups, a tutor, face-to-face sessions and new technology. These topics are covered with special attention to their implications for the writer of material: what does the writer need to produce to enable the package to be enhanced in these ways? Activities and checklists are included at appropriate points.

The place of this section in the book can be shown in the following way.

Source of feedback on progress	Comment
Self-assessment and activities.	The learner manages his own learning, using questions/responses within the package.
Self-help groups.	Learners meet together to discuss progress.
A person/persons.	A professional, eg, a tutor/trainer. A non-professional, eg, a colleague, member of the learner's family, another learner.
Face-to-face sessions.	Face-to-face meetings are used to provide the learner with feedback.
New technology.	New technology is used to provide the learner with feedback.

By working through this section you should be able to

— decide which of these means are open to you in your scheme
— decide what purposes any of these means could fulfil in your scheme
— produce material to facilitate the use of any of these means.

SELF-HELP GROUPS

On some courses learners can get together to discuss issues of interest. Groups might discuss, for example, assignments, SAQs, the results of activities, or aspects of the course that individuals have found difficult. If such groups exist they can provide an excellent means for individual learners to gain feedback on progress. You may consider writing guidelines on things such groups would discuss. Further advice is given later in this section and in the volume on *How to Tutor and Support Learners*.

It is also possible to encourage learners to use various other sources of help, eg, family, friends, colleagues at work, people in the community. See the examples from *Report Writing* and biology in the previous section. Professional educators and trainers are not always needed or indeed even desirable.

A TUTOR

Many open-learning schemes do nevertheless also make available a source of professional education or training help, a tutor. Sometimes such a person is local and accessible. But more often the tutor is distant from the learner.

```
FOR YOU          In what way is your need for 'new experiences'
TO DO            being met at the moment?




                 Did you include parts of the course in your list?
                 How many of your items are to do with work?  How
                 many with your personal life?  These are questions
                 that, at some stage, it might be profitable to
                 share with your supervisor.
```

Extract from the YMCA Certificate in Youth and Community Work. Workpack 1/1, sample learning materials, p 10. Published by the YMCA National College

The supervisors are experienced youth workers, recruited by recommendation. They are local to the students and meet their student each fortnight for one-and-a-half hours. The main role of the supervisor is to help the student to relate theory to practice and to develop as a practitioner. It is a non-didactic role but not a passive one.

Extract from 'The YMCA Distance-Learning Scheme' in 'Open Learning in Action' (Volume 1 in this series)

The rest of this section looks at the implications for the course writers of having a tutor provided at a distance from the learner, to mark work through the post.

Case-study
This situation is described in several of the case-studies in *Open Learning in Action*, eg, Clwyd, Zoo Animal Management, Doncaster (CET, 1984).

The section on the tutor is divided into four parts.

— What role will the distance tutor play in helping to assess progress?
— How can the writer produce effective tutor-assessed questions (TAQs)?
— What extra material might the writer need to produce specially for the tutor?
— How can the use of tutor-assessed questions and tutor notes be monitored?

How to use the tutor
It is expensive to provide the services of a subject specialist. So the wise course writer will save his TAQs for those objectives which really *need* the tutor's professional skills. These might be:

— putting together a series of skills previously tested separately by SAQs (eg, writing an essay to check that the learner can spell, punctuate, plan, etc)
— giving examination practice
— testing complex or higher level objectives, eg, those requiring dialogue with the tutor.

TAQs also give the learner the chance to use the tutor as an individual learning consultant. The learner, for example, can add a note mentioning any difficulties he is having with the course. The tutor can answer these when he replies and set any further reading or additional exercises that he thinks might help the learner to progress.

What does my tutor do?
We view your relationship with your tutor as very important. He will not only 'mark your work' but will guide and advise you throughout the course. You should always drop him a note when you are in difficulties and, where necessary, ask for help (e.g. whether or not you should do the optional extra sections). His job is to give you *personal* guidance. We hope that you will enter into a dialogue with your tutor, replying to any comments and questions on your work.

We tell you when we want you to send work to your tutor. It is indicated by the sign W Sometimes we ask you to carry out a piece of work and keep it by you ready to send to your tutor at the end of the block; at other times we ask you to carry out just one piece of work all at once right at the end of the block. These pieces of work for your tutor are important. They give your tutor a chance to give you individual help and give you the chance to write down further questions and problems for your tutor to answer. Try to send work in *regularly* to your tutor.

Extract from 'Preparing for Social Science' by L Maynard and R Lewis, p 18, National Extension College, 1981

> I don't know how to organize this answer properly. I have a feeling
> that I get rather off the point round about the fourth paragraph -
> could you advise?

A learner asks the tutor for help

> A tip or two about things to watch out for in the *next* assignment
> helps.
>
> A little criticism now and again of 'sticky patches' in the course
> material helps - the student feels that the tutor is on his/her 'side'.
>
> Students will often ask about problems with SAQs - it usually turns
> out that the printed SAQ response is either ambiguous, or not full
> enough.
>
> In general, I think that whatever points arise in a letter from tutor
> to student (domestic, general interest, work, etc) the student is
> looking for some sort of proof that the tutor *has read* the letter and
> not just the work.

A tutor comments on his role

If you know that a tutor will be provided for the course you are writing then
you may want to build in right from the start the possibilities for developing
the learner–tutor relationship.

How to write effective TAQs

First, as with SAQs, it's important to vary the TAQs you ask. In a useful
guide to 'Assessment', Nicola Durbridge lists the following types of TAQ
used in the Open University: open and unstructured essays, structured essays,
role-playing essays, interpretation of data, design, project, description of
processes, notes, definitions, hypotheses, calculations, sketches, critical re-
views. These are illustrated in Appendix 2. A social science example is chosen
but the ideas can be adapted to suit most other subjects.

Much of the advice given on writing good SAQs applies again to writing
TAQs. Relevant points can be quickly summarized.

Appropriate objectives should be covered.

The learners should be challenged at the correct level. There should not be
a quantum leap between SAQs and TAQs; rather the SAQs should lead
almost imperceptibly to the TAQ.

Full instructions should be given on how to answer, including advice on the
likely time an answer will take, with reassuring wording for learners who take
longer.

Questions should be clear and well-structured.

Encouragement and support should be built in — after all, this is common in well run conventional classes.

TAQs should be appropriately placed. They may be bound into the course material itself, printed in a supplement, or issued on separate sheets.

Place	Advantages	Disadvantages
1. In text	1. No separate pieces of paper to get lost. 2. Learners meet them at the right point in their studies.	1. Can be changed only when text reprinted (unless awkward errata slips used). Yet may need change for variety, etc.
2. In separate booklet	1. Easily updated/issued annually. 2. Convenient: all TMA material in one place. 3. Learner can see what's required of him throughout whole course.	1. Course writer may not want learner to see all TMAs at once; eg, may be daunting to student. 2. Cannot take into account learner feedback from earlier TMAs.
3. Issued separately	1. Flexible: can be written at short notice and using student feedback. 2. Learner gets TMA at time controlled by tutor/college/writer.	1. Learner cannot see year as a whole. 2. Someone will have to issue papers. 3. Papers may get lost.

They may be given to the learner all together at the start of the course or issued in stages.

Finally, they should be appropriately phased throughout the course of study. It is often a good idea to have an early first assignment to enable tutor and learner to establish easy contact. Assignments can be set at regular intervals, respecting such phenomena as holidays, busy times of the year (for learners and/or tutors) and the dates of any examinations.

Writing TAQs is not easy and it is important to spend time getting them right. You should involve others in the process:

— ask colleagues to read your questions in draft
— ask tutors to read them
— ask learners.

Ask your readers questions such as:

— is the purpose of the question clear
— is wording of the question clear
— are demands (time/level of difficulty) realistic
— will tutors find the questions interesting to mark?

Introduction

As you will see, this course is a mixture of study skills advice and training in things particularly relevant to science studies, such as graphs, error-handling, etc. The course is intended for students of very different levels, ie, from pre-O-level to postgraduate (eg, arts postgraduates venturing into the sciences for the first time). The course is also intended to help students following many different subject disciplines.

From the tutor's viewpoint, this means:

(a) the tutor may expect considerable variation in the standard of answers, reflecting both student experience and discipline
(b) the tutor will need to adjust his feedback comments and grading to the level and needs of each particular student
(c) from time to time the tutor may need to advise a student to skip any topics beyond capabilities or needs, and
(d) the tutor may expect general study-skills questions to be asked spontaneously by students.

I have written the assignment material to try to help the tutor in these tasks, particularly in questions where I hope to extract from each student an accurate picture of his/her particular circumstances, needs, and ambitions. Therefore, some of the assignments are so general that every student's answer will be quite different (although the tutor's role as I see it is simply to comment on the student's answer, and advise as he or she thinks fit). In assignments where definitive answers are possible I am providing model answers, with the intention that a copy of these answers should be returned to each student with marked work. In these notes, I comment briefly on my expectations of each assignment question.

Extract from 'Study Science Successfully: notes for tutors', National Extension College

Tutor notes

This section has concentrated on TAQs from the learner's perspective. But the course writer must also consider the tutor. The tutor must feel involved in the course to function successfully but this involvement is difficult to achieve when working from a distance. The tutor is distant not only from the learner but usually also from the processes of developing and writing the course. He may feel that he has lost some of his most cherished skills to a written package.

Thus the writer should, as far as he is able, help the tutor to feel committed to the course. How can he do this? Firstly, by setting questions which interest the tutor as well as the learner. Secondly, by recognizing and using the tutor's specialist skills. And thirdly by communicating with the tutor. The writer can, for example, produce 'tutor notes'. These can take the tutor behind the scenes, explain why particular topics were included and others omitted, outline the kinds of answers the course writer expected, and suggest ways in which learners can be helped by tutorial comment. 'Tutor notes' can be especially helpful to tutors new to this kind of work, though they would, ideally, be only a supplement to other forms of briefing and contact. Tutors like notes to answer such questions as

What did you have in mind when you wrote this assignment?

What do you intend it to test?

What would you expect the learner to cover in a 'model' answer?

How should variations on the model be handled?

What system of marking do you recommend? Which parts of the assignment merit the largest proportion of marks?

Monitoring TAQs and tutor notes

Once the course is running, TAQs and tutor notes should be monitored for effectiveness. Questions such as those listed on page 69 can be asked again and answered by a variety of means, such as records of learner performance and questionnaires. Each source of information will provide its own distinctive data.

Source	Examples of data
Course results	Did the TAQ produce more/less 'fails' than other TAQs?
Learners	How long did it take to answer the question? How interesting was the question?
Tutors	What were the main weaknesses in learners' answers? Did the question introduce any unnecessary difficulties? Did the answers reveal any problems in the course material? Were the tutor notes helpful?

You need to monitor not only individual TAQs but the TAQ programme as a whole, eg, did the difficulty level rise gradually enough? Were any assignments out of place in the sequence? Was the frequency right? Results might show the need to

— reschedule assignments
— reduce or increase the number of assignments in the course
— modify the advice and guidance given to learners on how to answer
— change the tutor notes or even modify the course material itself.

CNAA Postgraduate Diploma in Educational Technology

Course Assignment 3
COURSE DESIGN
GUIDELINES

Intake 6

We have only received a few submissions and drafts for this assignment but it is clear that many of you are omitting a key part of the assignment. You are asked to do two things:

— write a course proposal (as if for your employer or validating body).

— justify your decisions, particularly in terms of your chosen teaching methods.

DO NOT FORGET TO TACKLE BOTH PARTS OF THE ASSIGNMENT.

No matter how good your course proposal is, it will be returned for resubmission if you have not justified your ideas. It is not enough to mention the constraints of your institution. You should give reasons and arguments supporting your decisions. You could also say why you had not opted for certain other alternatives.

This is also useful training for your major project report where you will be expected to explain and justify your actions.

Extract from Dundee College of Educational Diploma in Educational Technology Cource Design module, 1983

Activity

Assuming your learners will have access to a tutor, decide what role the tutor will play in your scheme.

Decide what you can do to help the tutor carry out this role.

Are you responsible for writing assignments that tutors will mark?

If so, write some TAQs, using the checklist that follows to help you to assess your work.

Write tutor notes for the benefit of your tutors.

Decide where your TAQs will be placed in the text.

Checklist

Are you making sensible use of your tutor?

Do your TAQs consider the learner's perspective?

Are your TAQs:

— varied
— covering course objectives
— challenging but realistic
— clear
— well structured
— attractive and encouraging
— appropriately placed
— suitably spaced throughout the course?

Do your TAQs:

— include full instructions
— give study advice?

The tutor

Do your TAQs consider the tutor's perspective?

— Have you made him feel needed?
— Have you produced tutor notes?
— Have you made clear the initiative he can take?
— Will he be interested by your TAQs?
— Are your demands on his time realistic?

Piloting and monitoring

Have you made arrangements to pilot your TAQs and tutor notes?

Have you listed the questions you want your piloting to help you answer?

Have you made arrangements to monitor TAQs and tutor notes during the life of the course?

Have you listed the aspects you will monitor and made arrangements for the collection of relevant data?

Quiz

1. It is always essential to provide a tutor. True or false?

2. When a tutor marks a TAQ the learner gets feedback on how well he has answered. What else might he get that will help him?

3. One of your writers asks when he should set a SAQ and when a TAQ. What advice might you give?

4. Tutors, like learners, can feel isolated in open learning. Can you think of one way in which you might help tutors to feel involved?

5. Give one advantage and one disadvantage of binding TAQs into the text.

Answers

1. False. It depends on many things — content, objectives, learners, assessment arrangements. There are other ways of supporting learners than by recruiting a professional. *How to Tutor and Support Learners* (Volume 3 in this series) shows some of these.

2. Help with difficulties; his questions on the course material answered; human contact and encouragement; a spur to keep going — and other similar answers.

3. TAQs cover objectives that it is not so easy or appropriate to cover by SAQs, eg, a major objective, a synthesis of several objectives, objectives towards which the learner may have difficulty in assessing his own progress, objectives which require dialogue with another person. But your writer should remember that TAQs should always build from SAQs and that the TAQ should not be pitched at a level of difficulty for which the learner is unprepared.

4. You might:

— provide tutor notes
— ask tutors' views on questions at draft stage
— ask tutors to write the questions and notes
— send out a newsletter
— ask tutors for reports on how TAQs perform
— follow other similar, procedures.

5. Advantages: they won't get lost; learners meet them at the appropriate place in the study sequence. Disadvantage: it's hard to change them easily.

FACE–TO–FACE SESSIONS
If learners are distant from the providing centre then problems can arise with assessment. It may, for example, be difficult for the learner to assess how well he is mastering certain skills and practical operations. Some schemes deal with this

problem by calling learners together for occasional face-to-face sessions — such as Open University summer schools or the weekends described in the Doncaster quarrying case study. In such schemes the package writer may be required to provide checklists and other material to guide those present at the sessions.

Do you need such sessions?
What kinds of skills are not easy to assess by SAQs or activities or by a distant tutor? Here are some examples.

Notice the phrase 'not easy'. But it may be possible! Course planners sometimes assume that face-to-face contact is necessary when the relevant experience could actually be provided by some other means. Even a simple medium such as the audiocassette can be useful in assessing language skills across a distance, and a new medium such as interactive video makes it possible for the learner to assess his degree of success in practical skills (see the next section).

The best place for developing some of the skills could well be the learner's workplace. If, for example, you are assessing the counselling skills of social workers, then it would be best to set this in a context as near as possible to the one in which the skill will actually be used. The communication skill of a supervisor, or the ability of a secretary to operate a wordprocessor, will both be better assessed in the work environment than in a college classroom. And you would be saved the considerable inconvenience of having to set up special sessions.

It is important to distinguish between formal and informal assessment. Sometimes it is necessary for formal assessment to be carried out under controlled conditions. But this book is concerned with the informal feedback a learner needs to assess his progress for himself. This makes a variety of arrangements possible — for example, a highly qualified professional may not be needed; a sympathetic friend, counsellor, or colleague may be able to help the learner make the necessary appraisal, especially if provided with a checklist or other aid.

Specially organized sessions

Nevertheless, on some courses it may be necessary to gather learners together in special sessions, perhaps to help them assess their progress in carrying out 'process skills' which do not lead to an end product such as negotiating, counselling, interviewing or conversing in a foreign language. If so, a useful aid is the checklist, which states the criteria against which the learner's performance can be measured.

Can the teacher:

   Swim two lengths of the pool in 1 minute?

   Perform 3 different strokes, one on his front, one on his back and one on his side?

   Remove outer clothes whilst treading water?

   Rescue a partner from deep water?

   Carry out artificial respiration correctly?

   When confronted with a staged accident rescue three casualties in an appropriate order?

   Without undue fuss escort a class from the coach to the poolside in a safe manner?

Extract from a checklist developed for a teachers' swimming course. (NB. Each of the tasks would be further analysed and subdivided.)

Case-study
See *Open Learning in Action* (CET, 1984) for how the YMCA and Doncaster schemes use face-to-face sessions.

A

Activity

List skills in your course which the learner may find it hard to assess on his own and which are not amenable to assessment by distant tutor or by new technology.

Design a checklist or other aid for the use of participants in face-to-face sessions.

C

Checklist

Can you use your package to carry out informal assessment even of practical and interactive skills?

Can you arrange for the learners' skills to be assessed in a familiar and accessible place at work?

Can you arrange for learners to work in self-help groups?

Is it possible to call learners together in specially arranged face-to-face sessions? If so, how regularly and how frequently?

Will any such face-to-face sessions be run by
— subject specialists
— a counsellor, convenor or study adviser?

What facilities will be available? (Rooms, hardware, etc.) What use can you make of them?

Can you help whoever is present by issuing a checklist or other aids?

NEW TECHNOLOGY

So far I have looked at feedback via self-assessment questions and activities, feedback from a distant tutor and feedback from face-to-face sessions. But you may also be able to use new technology to provide learners with information on their progress. It is increasingly possible to link together different kinds of equipment in different locations. Information can be input at one place, processed and retrieved at quite a different place and in quite a different form. The costs of relevant equipment are also dropping. How can these developments help the open learner? This section considers a range of current and future possibilities.

Using computers

First, the medium for the presentation of learning material may itself be a computer. In this case, feedback is an integral part of the package and takes place as the learner works through the material. The computer presents questions which the learner answers by keying in an appropriate number or word. The computer then selects and generates the appropriate response. It may also present the learner with statistics on his performance. The computer thus makes possible sophisticated, rapid and direct feedback. At the time of writing this use of a computer is not widespread in open learning; none of the case studies in Volume 1 of this series makes any such use of the computer. But this situation is likely to change very quickly.

Secondly, the learner may work through a package presented in some other medium but go to a computer to take a test. Feedback may then either be displayed directly on the screen or given to the learner in some other medium (probably print) or be mediated by a tutor.

Thirdly, the computer can be used as a marking device. In this case the learner need have no access himself to a computer. He simply completes the answers on paper and sends them to a tutor or centre where they are fed into a computer either by keying or by some other means such as optical mark reader or light pen. The computer then produces results which are sent or passed to the learner. The Open University has used computer marking in this way for many years. The system can be crude and oriented towards formal assessment (as was the case in the early years of the Open University) or it can be much more sophisticated and aim at feedback and learner support, as with the systems known as CADE and RSVP. Since this book is concerned with providing feedback to learners rather than with assessing them I shall now discuss a feedback system.

MAIL

MAIL may be of particular interest to readers of this book since it can be added on to any existing or planned open-learning scheme, it is cheap to operate and it is very flexible. Furthermore the learner himself needs no hardware other than a pen or pencil — and he can work from home.

In MAIL the learner answers a series of multiple-choice questions by filling in a card or form. He then posts this to a central point to be marked by a microcomputer (BBC Model B). The system is described in the following article, 'Pop it in the post' by Karen Gold in *The Times Higher Educational Supplement* of 15 April 1983.

'Computerized letters, in common experience, arrive at least once a week announcing that you and you alone (plus everyone else in the telephone book) have been singled out for this special attention.

But for distance-learning students and tutors, computer-written letters may spell the answer to a previously intractable problem of their kind of study: keeping the student motivated to the end of the course.

The letters are sent out by a system called MAIL: micro-aided computer learning. They cover two pages of A4 paper, chattily praising right answers to a test assignment, correcting wrong ones, and suggesting ways and exercises to avoid the same mistakes again. They are personally addressed to the student and "signed" by the tutor.

Yet they are entirely written by a small BBC microcomputer, printed out almost quicker than the eye can read, and — galling for conscientious tutors — the students actually prefer them to assessment and advice by human markers!

Research carried out in Scandinavia in recent years has established that distance-learning (correspondence courses) students need to hear from their tutors no more than six days after carrying out an assignment for them.

After waiting six days, the students — notoriously isolated, mainly occupied with other activities than study, and easily discouraged — are no longer interested in their last essay or test, and therefore unable to build upon any comments or advice they eventually receive back with it.

Yet the conventional marking system, whereby the work goes from student to tutor, to college for registration and then back to the student, plus the vagaries of the postal service, mean few students receive their work back in under 10, and more often, 14 days.

Cutting down that time by using multiple-choice tests and computer-marking the answers is nothing new: the Open University has done it for years. But the use to a student of a series of "ticks and crosses" type marking is recognized by the OU as much as anyone; hence their balance between computer-marked and tutor-marked assignments.

Under the MAIL system, the assignment can leave the student on Monday, be at the college Tuesday morning, marked and in the out-tray again by 10 am and back with the student in time for breakfast on Wednesday. Even allowing for weekends and Post Office delays, there is a huge margin between that and the six-day deadline.

The system has been introduced into this country by the Cambridge-based National Extension College. Its director, Richard Freeman, spent two years trying to persuade colleges and mainframe computer manufacturers to take it on; eventually, having raised no enthusiasm, he realized the whole thing could go on a microcomputer and decided the NEC should do it itself.

The NEC is currently using it for its combined numeracy course with television: "Make it Count". It will be available to other distance-learning course organizers from September and has already aroused wide interest from colleges and polytechnics.

It is typical of the potential in "the bargain basement level of information technology", which holds out exciting prospects but also severe dangers for distance learning, Mr Freeman told a recent conference on continuing education.

Open learning was about three things, he said: students learning what they wanted, not what institutions wanted them to learn; students learning when they wanted, rather than to an imposed timetable; and students learning where they wanted to be, not where other people — or the availability of expensive technology — dictated.

From this followed three principles for applying information technology to open learning. The first was that it made possible something that could not be done before, such as the very fast feedback of the MAIL system or the new systems of teaching typing or tables and fractions to children.

All of those involved tedious, repetitive tasks, which by using simple technology — sometimes just cassette tapes — could release staff for more worthwhile work. The MAIL system may soon be adaptable for writing reports instead of letters, which would make far easier another repetitious task.

His second principle was that something done with IT could be done cheaper than otherwise, and that saving could be passed on to the learner. The third was that IT could offer greater flexibility, perhaps eventually writing courses in such a way that learners could pick out the parts they wanted.

The most important thing about the MAIL system was that the learners needed no access to any technology at all, he said. "No FE college is going to have 8000 visual display units."

It was very cheap — £2000 — it was easy for tutors to use — they simply have to write in the replies they want printed out for no more than four possible answers, a, b, c or d, to no more than 10 questions for one assignment — and they could add on to it without disturbing the existing course.

Each course can have up to 15 of these tests. For each test the tutor constructs a personalized letter from a series of comments, and has to specify the number of questions, the number of blocks — the test can be subdivided into one to three blocks — the correct response letter for each question, the score for each response, block questions and block comments.'

'Pop it in the Post' by Karen Gold, 'The Times Higher Educational Supplement', 15 April 1983

There are clear advantages in using a system of this kind.

Advantages over SAQs	The learner has to answer in order to get a response, ie, 'cheating' is impossible; the response is concealed.
	The response is individualized; it takes into account the response of that particular learner.
Advantages over TAQs	It is quicker for the learner to answer multiple-choice questions.
	The learner gets the feedback quicker than from a tutor.
	The feedback is more detailed than that provided by most tutors.
	The system is reliable and consistent: tutors vary in their standards and an individual tutor's performance will vary according to how he feels and how much time he has available.
	MAIL is impersonal and some learners like this. It is very cheap; once the questions and responses are prepared it is something between five and 16 times cheaper than using a tutor.

SAQs and TAQs do, of course, themselves have some advantages over systems like MAIL.

SAQ advantages	The response is even quicker.
	The learner has more control; can choose whether or not to answer.
	SAQs are more flexible.
	SAQs are more private.
TAQ advantages	TAQs are better for assessing certain skills, eg, the production of continuous prose.
	The tutor can conduct a unique, personal dialogue.
	The tutor can deal with other problems raised by the learner, eg, in a letter accompanying an assignment.

The moral is obvious. The wise course designer and writer will use a mixture of assessment methods to capitalize on the strengths of each.

It is important to point out that writing questions for use in MAIL requires special skills, ideally developed in a one- to two-day workshop. For more information on this or other aspects of MAIL write to the NEC Open Learning Unit, 20 Forehill, Ely, Cambs CB7 4AF.

Likely future developments
This section on technology will already be out of date by the time this book is published. As I write, MAIL is itself undergoing extensive modification to meet new needs such as diagnosis of learner capacities. The following are other likely developments of relevance to this text.

Interactive video
This is a new and exciting conjunction of microcomputer and videodisc or videocassette. Interactive video couples the sophisticated immediate response of a computer with the visual clarity of a video picture. It is important for us here because it enables instant feedback on practical skills to be given to the learner without the intervention of a tutor. In Scandinavia, for example, all new subway drivers train in a simulator which gives a video picture of the route which moves faster or slower depending on the speed of the train. Obstacles and hazards can be generated by the computer to test the driver's reactions without him actually having to put himself or the train in any danger.

Telephone and computer
Systems now exist whereby a learner can receive a program 'page by page' on his home television screen, linked to a microcomputer. This technique is known as 'telesoftware'. Answers to questions on the material can be transmitted to a central computer via a telephone line for feedback; solutions can in some systems be downloaded back to the home.

Cable

Advanced cable systems such as fibre optics will bring greater potential for interactive communication between users and system. British Telecom is developing an 'interactive video library system' which combines computers, interactive video and the fibre optic communication network. A pilot will be running in Merseyside.

Some of these developments will be widely used by the time this book is read. They are all based on technologies that actually exist. What is less certain is whether course designers and writers will use them to the full.

For more information on these and other developments contact the Information Officer at the Council for Educational Technology, 3 Devonshire Street, London W1N 2BA.

 Checklist

What technology can you call on?

What function can this play in your course?

Can you and/or the learners gain easy access to it?

Do you and/or the learners need to acquire skills to operate the technology?

How can any necessary operating skills and attitudes be acquired?

Have you the financial resources and time to develop and use the technology?

What future developments are relevant to your needs?

Can you find out more about them?

Section Four. Checklists, Booklist and Glossary

Checklists

The checklists given at various points of the book are gathered together here. You can use them:

— as an entry point to the book
— to reinforce your earlier work on the sections
— to deal with specific problems and issues as they arise in your scheme.

Don't be put off by the number of items listed. You need select only those of relevance to your own context. The questions would in practice arise during a period of weeks or months and would probably be tackled by a team rather than by just one individual.

CHECKLISTS
Objectives
Look back over your objectives. Are the verbs that begin them precise enough?

What form of objectives do you need in order to communicate
— between yourselves
— to learners?

Which of the three types of objective discussed in the text is or are most important for your own course? (Thinking, doing, feeling.)

Have you covered a wide enough range of objectives?

Have you paid enough attention to the development of attitudes, feelings and skills as well as knowledge?

Take your list of objectives and see how well they stand up to the following questions. Revise any that seem unsatisfactory, but remember that you are seeking workable rather than perfect objectives. You can always go back to modify the objectives after you have drafted some of your text.

Does each objective begin with a verb?

Is the learning outcome described exactly enough?

Is the learning outcome significant and relevant?

Does each objective describe one outcome only?

Does each objective respect the expertise and experience of the learner?

Is each objective attainable and realistic?

Are the objectives grouped in manageable ways? In particular, have you avoided over-long lists of objectives?

Is each objective clearly phrased?

Are your objectives phrased appropriately to the target audience?

Does each objective lead easily to a related assessment item? (See Section Two of this book.)

Are your objectives written consistently to whatever format has been chosen?

Are your objectives varied in range and complexity?

Have you shown your objectives to other people for comment?

You may also like to refer to Appendix 1 which summarizes the qualities of a sound objective.

Self-assessment questions

Does each SAQ relate to an objective of your course?

Have you tested each and every objective? Once or twice?

Are your SAQs attractive? Will the learner want to answer them?

Is it clear how each SAQ will help the learner?

Are your SAQs realistic? Will the learner be able to answer them?

Have you divided long and complex questions into shorter and simpler ones?

Are your SAQs varied in type? Tick which of the following you have used.

Those where everything is given	*Those where the learner must supply an answer*
MCQ	One word
Matching list	List
True/false	Phrase
Putting points in a sequence or hierarchy	Sentence
	Paragraph
Blank spaces with words, etc, provided from which the learners must select	Plan
	Case-study with questions
Drawing a graph	Drawing a graph
	Practical SAQ

Are your SAQs varied in length and nature of answer/outcome?

Is the learner given a clear indication of the length and type of answer expected?

Are your SAQs frequent enough? Is an SAQ always in sight?

Are your SAQs clearly constructed?

Are your SAQs written in clear language? Are there any difficult words that might be unfamiliar to the learner?

Have you provided any study advice necessary to help the learner to answer?

Do your SAQs clearly stand out? Have you used a symbol or other convention to identify them?

Have you provided an answer or response to each SAQ?

Are your answers clear?

Have you reinforced the correct answer?

Have you given guidance on wrong answers?

Have you explained how the correct answer is arrived at?

Have you referred to other parts of the course?

Have you set follow-up work?

Are your responses of an appropriate length?

Are your responses in an appropriate place?

Have you considered the learners' feelings — eg, congratulated learners on correct answers; sympathized with learners who make mistakes that are common?

NB. Not every question will apply to every case. Select, and attend to, those which are relevant to you.

Activities

Does your activity relate to an objective of your course?

Is your activity attractive? Will the learner want to try it?

Are the purposes of your activity clear?

Is your activity realistic in the demands it makes on the learner?

Have you structured your activity in such a way that the learners can tackle it?

Is the likely outcome of your activity indicated?

Have you given any necessary advice to the learners on how to carry out the activity?

Are your activities varied?

Have you used enough activities?

Do your activities clearly stand out in the package? Have you used a symbol or some other convention to identify them?

Have you borne any safety considerations in mind?

Have you referred your learner to further sources of help either inside or outside the package?

Using a tutor for assessment
Are you making sensible use of your tutor?

Do your TAQs consider the learner's perspective?

Are your TAQs:

— varied
— covering course objectives
— challenging but realistic
— clear
— well structured
— attractive and encouraging
— appropriately placed
— suitably spaced throughout the course?

Do your TAQs:

— include full instructions
— give study advice?

Do your TAQs consider the tutor's perspective?
— Have you made him feel needed?
— Have you produced tutor notes?
— Have you made clear the initiatives he can take?
— Will he be interested by your TAQs?
— Are your demands on his time realistic?

Have you made arrangements to pilot your TAQs and tutor notes?

Have you listed the questions you want your piloting to help you answer?

Have you made arrangements to monitor TAQs and tutor notes during the life of the course?

Have you listed the aspects you will monitor and made arrangements for the collection of relevant data?

Using face-to-face sessions for assessment
Can you use your package to carry out informal assessment even of practical and interactive skills?

Can you arrange for the learners' skills to be assessed in a familiar and accessible place at work?

Can you arrange for learners to work in self-help groups?

Is it possible to call learners together in specially arranged face-to-face sessions? If so, how regularly and how frequently?

Will any such face-to-face sessions be run by
— subject specialists
— a counsellor, convenor or study adviser?

What facilities will be available? (Rooms, hardware, etc.) What use can you make of them?

Can you help whoever is present by issuing a checklist or other aids?

Using new technology for assessment
What technology can you call on?

What function can this play in your course?

Can you and/or the learners gain easy access to it?

Do you and/or the learners need to acquire skills to operate the technology?

How can any necessary operating skills and attitudes be acquired?

Have you the financial resources and time to develop and use the technology?

What future developments are relevant to your needs?

Can you find out more about them?

Booklist

OBJECTIVES
For practical help
Mager, Robert J, *Preparing Instructional Objectives*, Fearon, 1962
Royal Air Force School of Education, *A Guide to the Writing of Objectives* (2 vols) (no date, not generally available)
Russell, T J, *A Workshop on the Writing of Learning Objectives*, Coombe Lodge Working Paper 1331, Further Education Staff College, Coombe Lodge, Blagdon, Bristol, 1979

For a more philosophical treatment
Davies, Ivor K, *Objectives in Curriculum Design*, McGraw-Hill, 1976
Gagné, Robert M and Briggs, Leslie J, *Principles of Instructional Design*, Holt, Rinehart and Winston, 1974

If you are in schools then you may find these useful
Bloom, B, *Handbook of Formative and Summative Evaluation of Student Learning*, McGraw-Hill, 1971
Gronlund, Norman E, *Stating Behavioural Objectives for Classroom Instruction*, Macmillan, 1970

If you are in training then you may find this useful
Dean, Christopher and Whitlock, Quentin, *A Handbook of Computer-Based Training*, Kogan Page, 1983

ASSESSMENT
For further practical help on SAQs
Paine, Nigel, *How to Write Self-Assessment Questions*, SCET Open Learning Paper No. 402, Scottish Council for Educational Technology, 1983

For further practical help on MCQs
City and Guilds of London Institute, *The Manual of Objective Testing*, 1977
Russell, T J, *A Workbook on the Writing and Evaluation of Multiple-Choice Items*, Coombe Lodge Workbook No. 1330, 1979
Stratton, N J, 'Recurrent faults in objective test items' in *Teaching at a Distance* No. 20 (pp 66–72), Open University, 1981

For assessment more generally
Gronlund, Norman E, *Management and Evaluation in Teaching*, Macmillan, 1971
Rowntree, Derek, *Assessing Students. How shall we know them?* Harper and Row, 1977

For computer feedback systems

Baker, Michael, 'The fast feedback system' in *Teaching at a Distance* No. 24, Open University, 1983
Freeman, Richard, 'MAIL from the NEC' in *Teaching at a Distance* No. 24, Open University, 1983
Mullett, Tony, 'Feedback on T101' in *Teaching at a Distance* No. 24, Open University, 1983

Glossary

Activity. An opportunity to apply learning to the world outside the package.

Aim. A general statement of the intention of the planner or writer. (See *Objective.*)

Assignment. A piece of work completed by a learner and handed or sent to a tutor for comment and assessment (also called TAQ, *Tutor-assessed question*).

Case-study. Presentation of real or imagined experience often, in an open-learning package, followed by self-assessment questions.

Checklist. A list of questions against which a learner can check progress towards carrying out a particular activity.

Course. A planned learning experience. It may be tightly structured (eg, the Open University undergraduate programme) or loose (eg, a study circle); it may be long or short in duration; it may or may not lead to a qualification; it may be offered by an educational, industrial or other provider; it may be formal or informal. In industry the word *programme* is sometimes used instead of *course.* In this book *scheme* and *project* are used synonymously with *course.*

Feedback. The provision of comment on a learner's performance either within the package or by some other means (eg, computer; tutor). In the package this may be called 'answer', 'response' or some similar name.

MAIL. An abbreviation of Micro Aided Learning, a computerized system developed by the National Extension College in 1983 to provide fast feedback for open learners.

Matching list. A question which presents two lists for the learner who has to match items in one list with those in the other.

Monitoring. The regular scrutiny of the performance of the scheme, or part of a scheme, as it is running; checking the effectiveness or management procedures, learner support and learning materials. Often used more interchangeably with *evaluation.*

Multiple-choice question (MCQ). A question which takes the form of a stem followed by a series of possible answers (options). Usually only one of these is correct (the key) and others are incorrect (the distractors).

Objective. A description of the purpose of a course expressed in terms of the capacities that the learner will acquire and demonstrate; a statement of learning outcome. See *Aim.*

Open-learning/course/programme/scheme/system. 'Open learning' is a term used to describe courses flexibly designed to meet individual requirements. It is often applied to provision which tries to remove barriers that prevent attendance at more traditional courses but it also suggests a learner-centred philosophy. Open-learning courses may be offered in a learning centre of some kind or most of the activity may be carried out away from such a centre (eg, at home). See Volume 4 of this series, *What is open learning?* Note that *course, project, scheme* and *system* are synonymous.

Open-learning package/package/materials/materials. Specially prepared or adapted materials to enable the learner to study for a significant part of his time on his own.

Pilot. The trial of a *scheme* or part of it before full operation, with the intention of collecting feedback, to assess its performance and decide on any modification necessary; *validation, trial, test* and *try out* are used synonymously with *pilot.*

Self-assessment question (SAQ). An opportunity that enables the learner to prepare for a learning experience; tests his understanding of a particular point; enters into dialogue with the course writer.

Self-help group. A group of learners who came together voluntarily to plan and implement a learning programme. Their objectives may be preset (eg, a syllabus) or formulated by the learners themselves.

Telesoftware. The transmission of digital information, programs and data from one computer to another. Telesoftware may be broadcast via radio or television (as part of a teletext service) or via cable including the public switched telephone network.

Tutor. General term for the person in an open-learning system who is directly responsible for the learner. The tutor is usually a professional — an educator or trainer. His main task is to help the learner to acquire skills and strategies needed to become autonomous, usually through mastery of a particular subject area or skill. He is variously described as 'counsellor', 'mentor', 'coach', 'guide', 'trainer', 'supervisor' and 'godfather'.

Tutor-assessed question (TAQ). see *Assignment.*

Tutor notes. Instructions, guidance, etc, provided by a course writer to help tutors carry out their role in an open-learning scheme.

Target audience. The learners for whom a particular course has been prepared.

Appendices

-12-

6. Project

Assemble a file of items, e.g. newspaper cuttings, results of an interview with local planners and businessmen which you might conduct yourself, relating to a piece of proposed or completed redevelopment and its possible effects on property and land values. Include your assessment of the problems as you learn more about them.

7. Description of Processes

Define the term 'Externalities' as used by an economist. Select a land use with both positive and negative externalities and describe the influence of these activities upon each other and upon urban land values.

8. Notes

List some of the public services which are determinants of the value of an individual site or property; in note form then discuss some of the other kinds of public services which may influence land values generally.

9. Definitions

Define the following terms –

Property rights in land

Zoning

Imputed rent

Externalities

Betterment

Access

Accessibility

10. Hypotheses

Suggest the relationships between nearby house prices and

a) the development of a new shopping precinct in a suburban area.

b) a road widening scheme in the same area

11. Calculation

Given the formula: $M = \sum_{all\ i} \frac{Qi}{Tc}$

and the two sets of values:-

a).... b).....

Where M = Market potential for

Firm X sited in the city centre

Qi = potential market in area i and

Ti = transport cost between the firms location and area i;

Appendix 1. Summary: good and bad objectives

Strong features	Weak features
Describe learner outcome eg, to list three main principles of marketing	Refer to teacher behaviour eg, to cover the main principles the teacher will lead a discussion on the main principles of marketing
Are specific eg, given a format, can produce a marketing plan for a new product	Are general eg, understand about planning and marketing for a new product
Describe observable outcomes eg, states three reasons why the small businessman must consider marketing	Describe states of mind eg, understands why marketing is important
Describe behaviour eg, list three main principles of marketing	Describe subject matter eg, the main principles of marketing
Builds on the strengths of the learners as identified at the course planning stage eg, apply the three principles to your own business	Ignore existing strengths of learners
Clear; concise eg, list three ways in which you promote a product	Ambiguous; wordy eg, explain some of the methods and strategies which a business may use in order to bring a particular and specified product to the knowledge of relevant and important sections of the public

Strong features	Weak features
Covers one outcome eg, (1) identify the information you require to... (2) locate the information	Covers several outcomes eg, identify and locate the information you require to...
Leads easily to an assessment item eg, the following objective recognizes three reasons why the small businessman must consider marketing leads to: — the following are five reasons given for marketing. Tick the three that, according to the author, are the most important.	No clear and easy path to an assessment item eg, understands why marketing is important leads to where?

It is not easy to show 'good' and 'bad' examples of objectives in the abstract. Much depends, of course, on the nature of each scheme and in particular on the characteristics of the learners.

Appendix 2. Writing tutor-assessed questions

```
         -11-
A survey in 1974  found the following types of TMAs in use:
1. Standard essay  'Land values are both the product and
                    the determinant of the pattern of urban
                    development' Discuss.
2. Structured essay
                    Identify and discuss some of the
                    determinants of urban land values and
                    their impact on urban development.  In
                    your answer you should -
                    a) define the following terms:-
                        i)    Property rights in land
                        ii)   Zoning
                        iii)  Site value rating
                    b) explain the influence of these
                        terms on determining land values
                    c) select i)   one activity of
                                   public authorities,
                        and ii)    one market factor, which
                        affect land values and explain how it
                        might influence urban development.
3. Role-playing essay
                    You have inherited your late uncle's
                    urban estate under his will and are
                    considering whether it would be more
                    profitable to sell the property quickly
                    or 'sit and speculate'.  Describe some of
                    the factors as discussed in Unit 14 you
                    would consider in making your decision.
4. Interpretation of Data
                    You own a house in a developing suburban
                    area but are considering selling your
                    property and moving closer to the city
                    centre.  Given the following Demographic
                    data:-.......... What are some of the
                    economic and social factors which you'd
                    consider in coming to a decision?
5. Design
                    As a town planner you are involved with
                    the design and siting of a new small
                    shopping precinct.  You favour a site
                    which involves the demolition of an old
                    street in the city centre.  Consider the
                    possible effects on land value and access-
                    ibility of such redevelopment and present
                    an argument for such a siting.
```

-13-

1) Measure the market potentials
   for a) and b) and compare their
   relative values.

2) The two measures of accessibility
   described in the text are not often
   used to explain land values. Why are
   such calculations less than satisfactory?

12. 'Sketch'   The map reproduced below shows X town
               with some of its major facilities:
               e.g. the main roads traversing it

                       the railway line
                       the siting of the parks
                       the canal.

               The two lines A-B and C-D cross this city

               Plot two graphs for A-B and C-D to
               represent the likely office development
               land values and their fluctuations across
               the town.

13. Critical Review
               Give a reasoned critique of Henry
               George's thesis that a tax on property
               rights in land is a remedy for the problems
               caused by increasing rents. State whether
               or not you agree with his conclusions and
               give your reasons for the view you put
               forward.

Extract from '1974 TMAs and the Preliminary Groupings' by Nicola Durbridge, Institute of Educational Technology, The Open University, unpublished

Appendix 3. Writing multiple-choice questions

This is reprinted with permission from *How to Develop Self-Instructional Teaching*, edited by Derek Rowntree and Brendan Connors and published by the Open University in 1979. The extract offers three guidelines, each of which is subdivided as follows.

Guideline	Example of sub-points
The item should communicate clearly	No confusing words; concise; grammatically coherent; alternatives all of the same kind; no negatives; use of visual material when relevant; logical
The distractors should distract and the preferred answer should not call attention to itself	No obviously wrong (eg, far-fetched) distractors
The item should include no unintentional clues	The preferred answer should not be longer than the distractors

Examples of the guidelines are given in the text.

I should also remind you of two further points, not covered in the Appendix but particularly relevant where questions are used primarily for feedback rather than for assessment:

— the distractors should represent anticipated or proven directions of learner error

— where *feedback* is the purpose of the MCQs (rather than testing) the distractors should represent cases where genuine help can be given to the learners choosing them.

First guideline: The item should communicate what is intended
                 as clearly as possible.

Is the style in which it is written as simple and
straightforward as possible?

POOR	BETTER
Which of the following urban centres possesses a university founded in the Middle Ages	Which city has an ancient University
A York	A York
B Canterbury	B Canterbury
C Oxford	C Oxford
D Winchester	D Winchester

Does the item contain any word or phrase which is not
important to what is being tested, but which might
confuse students who would otherwise be able to
answer correctly?

POOR	BETTER
Which is the eponymous hero of a Dickens novel	Which is both the hero and the title of a Dickens novel
A Ebenezer Scrooge	A Ebenezer Scrooge
B Nicholas Nickleby	B Nicholas Nickleby
C Wilkins Mickawber	C Wilkins Mickawber
D Sam Weller	D Sam Weller

Is the item as concise as possible?

POOR	BETTER
Which vegetable substance is the raw material for the manufacture of linen goods	Linen is made from
A Jute	A Jute
B Cotton	B Cotton
C Flax	C Flax
D Hemp	D Hemp

Is the wording of the alternatives repetitious?
If so, can common elements be transferred to the
stem?

POOR	BETTER
Where is Antwerp situated	Antwerp is on the river
A On the river Rhine	A Rhine
B On the river Maas	B Maas
C On the river Elbe	C Elbe
D On the river Scheldt	D Scheldt

Are the alternatives gramatically parallel?

POOR	BETTER
Psephology takes an interest in	Psephology takes an interest in
A Studies of early Egypt	A Studying early Egypt
B The categorisation of families of insects	B Categorising families of insects
C Wherever Biblical studies can be brought up to date	C Updating Biblical studies
D The way people vote in elections	D Studying voting patterns in elections

Are the alternatives all of the same kind?

POOR	BETTER
Chaucer wrote	Chaucer wrote a number of
A In Norman French	A Epic poems
B In the 12th century	B Political sonnets
C Some coarse anecdotes	C Coarse anecdotes
D On clay tablets	D Short novels

Does the item contain unnecessary (and possibly
confusing) negatives?

POOR	BETTER
In which town is it not an unnecessary precaution to avoid unboiled drinking water	In which town is it best to boil drinking water
A London	A London
B Calcutta	B Calcutta
C New York	C New York
D Sydney	D Sydney

Can the item be made clearer by including visual
material - diagrams, charts, etc?

POOR	BETTER
The space between two circles which are concentric, but of different radii, is called	The shaded area is referred to by name
A An annulus	A annulus
B A torus	B torus
C A sector	C sector
D A segment	D segment

Can the alternatives be placed in a logical (eg
numerical) order?

POOR	BETTER
The Battle of Waterloo took place in	The Battle of Waterloo took place in
A 1815	A 1798
B 1805	B 1805
C 1812	C 1812
D 1798	D 1815

Second guideline: The 'distractors' should distract, and the
                   preferred answer should not draw attention to itself.

Are any of the distractors obviously wrong to an
intelligent student?

POOR

Suriname is in

A   South America
B   Indonesia
C   India
D   Shropshire

BETTER

Suriname is in

A   South America
B   Indonesia
C   India
D   East Africa

Are any of the distractors so far-fetched or strangely
worded as to be meaningless to students?

POOR

The basis of living tissue
is sometimes known as

A   Protoplasm
B   Lymph
C   Cerebral cortex
D   Primordial utricle

BETTER

The basis of living tissue
is sometimes known as

A   Protoplasm
B   Lymph
C   Cerebral cortex
D   Haemoglobin

Is one alternative an instance of, or included in,
another?

POOR

The quickest way to travel
between Heathrow and Gatwick
airports is by

A   Road
B   Rail
C   Air
D   Helicopter

BETTER

The quickest way to travel
between Heathrow and Gatwick
airports is by

A   Road
B   Rail
C   Jet aircraft
D   Helicopter

Third guideline: The item should contain no unintended clues.

Is the preferred answer much longer or more detailed
than the distractors?

POOR	BETTER
One of the most common causes of piston trouble is	One of the most common causes of piston trouble is
A Warped pistons	A Warped pistons
B Piston slap	B Piston slap
C Excessive deposit of hard carbon on the pistons	C Carbonised pistons
D Scored pistons	D Scored pistons

Are all the alternatives consistent with whatever
indefinite article - 'a' or 'an' - used in the stem?

POOR	BETTER
The unit of electric current is an	Which is the unit of electric current?
A ampere	A ampere
B volt	B volt
C watt	C watt
D decibel	D decibel

LOOK FOR THE CLUES - A CONTENT-FREE TEST

Select one response for each item -   Time Allowed: Not more than 15 mins
only one is correct

1. The usual function of grunge-prowlers is to remove -

    A.   Grunges

    B.   Snarts

    C.   Trigs

    D.   Grods.

2. Antigrottification occurs -

    A.   On spring mornings

    B.   On summer evenings, provided there is no rain before dusk

    C.   On autumn afternoons

    D.   On winter nights.

3. Lurkies suffer from trangitis because -

    A.   Their prads are always underdeveloped

    B.   All their brizes are horizontal

    C.   Their curnpieces are usually imperfect

    D.   None of their dringoes can ever adapt.

4. Non-responsive frattling is usually found in an -

    A.   Gringle

    B.   Janket

    C.   Kloppie

    D.   Uckerpod.

5. Which are the exceptions to the law of lompicality -

    A.   The miltrip and the nattercup

    B.   The bifid pantrip

    C.   The common queeter

    D.   The flanged ozzer.

6. Which must be present for parbling to take place -

    A.   Phlot and runge

    B.   Runge

    C.   Stuke and runge

    D.   Runge and trake.

7. One common disorder of an overspragged uckerpod is -

    A.   Copious vezzling

    B.   Intermittent weggerment

    C.   Non-responsive frattling

    D.   Uneven yerkation.

8. Which one of these is right, A, B, C, or D?

NOTE: The answers to this test appear on the next page.

ANSWERS TO CONTENT-FREE TEST

1.   A.   A cork-screw removes corks; a bottle-opener opens bottles.
            Therefore a grunge-prowker removes grunges.

2.   B.   Any self-respecting academic will make sure he covers himself
            by qualifying any statement he makes. B is the only response
            with a proviso attached.

3.   C.   As for B above, one must cover oneself by avoiding sweeping
            generalisations; therefore "usually" is much more likely than
            "always", "all", and "none...ever".

4.   D.   The stem gives the clue. The correct response must start with a
            vowel because it is preceded by "an".

5.   A.   Again the stem gives the clue. The correct response must be
            plural to go with "are".

6.   B.   "Runge" is the only common element in the four responses; it
            seems a safe bet as the correct answer.

7.   C.   "Uckerpod" has occurred previously in the test, and so has
            "non-responsive frattling". Therefore it seems safe to assume
            that "non-responsive frattling" would not be completely out of
            context in relation to "uckerpod".

8.   D.   Any self-respecting test-writer makes sure that correct
            responses are well distributed: there have been two A's, two
            B's, two C's, but only one D so far. Moreover, D completes
            the neat pattern of answers to the first seven questions:
            A, B, C, D, A, B, C... Alternatively, D is on the right.